DRAMA FREE DIVORCE DETOX

The True You

LOREN SLOCUM LAHAV

ISBN 978-1-909359-27-7

Published by:

MyVoice Publishing
33-34 Mountney Bridge Business Park
Westham
PEVENSEY
BN24 5NJ

Book & Cover Design by :

Shariar Ahmed
Momo Kunjo 1st Floor, Suit No 3,
376/D Agrabad Access Road,
Chittagong 4100, Bangladesh.
www.shariarahmed.com

TABLE OF CONTENTS

Acknowledgements

*M*y life has been blessed with people who make me a better person. If I were to list them all it would be a book unto itself. My appreciation goes out to all who have touched my life and whose sheer presence makes this world a better place!

First and foremost I need to acknowledge my kids. I pinch myself daily to make sure I'm not dreaming. They each have an amazing heart and are so full of love for those around them and the world they live in. It hasn't been easy for them but they have grown stronger and more centered.

Not only do I love them, I respect them!

Jos: Inspires me constantly with his honesty and awareness.

Quinn: Fuels me with his hugs, infectious laugh and his dedication.

Asher: Teaches me daily how to slow done, live life and enjoy every moment.

Z: Who inspired and encouraged me to write this book. Who would ever think that I would meet my future husband at

"Baggage Claim"? I love and respect him with all of my heart. He is now and will forever be my ROCK!

My hairy four legged sons: Mojo, our English Bulldog who brightens everyone's day with that baby face, Lego, my wise old soul Labrador and Buddy, our Labrador who has grown from being scared of his own shadow to a happy dog.

Shore: Father to my amazing children; who continues to be my dear friend. His creativity and passion always inspires me. Without him this book would have never been possible.

My Mom: Whom I have caused many sleepless years. I love, honor and admire her gentle strength and am grateful for our friendship.

My Dad: He is my guardian angel. Just know when you find a quarter; he is there to let you know everything is exactly how it needs to be.

My Brother: For always being RIGHT! His wife Heidi and my cool niece, Lila who Asher adores!

Iyanla Vanzant: A very REAL example of being REAL in the tough times. Every book she has ever written seems to come out when I needed them most.

My Las Vegas St Jude Fellow Board Members for the past 6 years: Tanya, Dorit, Heidi, Robyn, Noa, Mala, Carrie who truly confirm that selfless contribution heals.

My Las Vegas Friends: Arte, Tony and Vanessa for always making sure I am dressed to feel like ME...LOVE my Vasari!

My "I'm there for you Girlfriends": Marica, Patty, Suzie, Ina, Julie, Vivica, Karen, Andrea, Elizabeth, Christina and Olivia.

My Robbins road team: OH...the places we have been! Terri, Karl, Chili, Samu, Alex, Lisa, Jonathon, Jay, Sam, Jenn, Gary, Patty, Sara, Shari, Mike S and all the Crew that I have had the honor to work hand and hand with the past 24 years. The Senior Leadership and Trainers who motivate not only me but people all over the world.

My Juice Plus Family: Including Jay, Sandra Martin, Paolo, Elton, Chris and John, Simon, Dan, Peter, Louise, Lindy, Celine, Jeff, Cheryl and Team YOLO who are dedicated to the health and welfare of everyone they meet.

My Leadership Team NMDS on Team YOLO: Gerry, Linda, Susie and Lynda. Soon to be NMDS , Luke, Danielle, Joanie, Manon, Neha and Maia.

Dory: For giving me the gift of "Captivating: Unveiling the Mystery of a Woman's Soul" by John Eldredge and Stasi Eldredge.

My forever friends: Near or far, words cannot convey my love and loyalty for Joelle, Jenn, Courtney, Dalyce, Heidi, Toni, Tina, Sissy, Wendy, Chris, Anne, Jayne, Tani, Suzanne, Michele, Stephanie, Phillip, Jamie, Kevin, Tony, JR, Adam, Philippe, Amber, Melody and Jon.

Tony and Sage Robbins: Who never waiver in their support and encouragement. I am forever thankful for my 45th birthday present in Israel...The Story Process.

Michele: For understanding ME and my message!

And to each of you who trusted me to pick up this book!

About The Author

Loren Slocum Lahav is a kickass motivator for women around the world. A distinguished worldwide personal development seminar leader, international speaker, coach, author, philanthropist and entrepreneur who considers her role as "Mom" to Jos, Quinn and Asher to be her biggest accomplishment.

Loren is the "real deal" and believes that being real is the only true way to live your life. She uses her "realness" to help people find empowerment, recognize their value and to learn to stay true to who they are at their core. Through Drama Free Divorce Detox, Life Tune-ups and her organization Lobella International, Loren is a mentor to women globally. She is passionate about the three R's that she considers a constant necessity in life; rediscover, reclaim and reinvent.

Loren has facilitated hundreds of six day comprehensive programs for The Anthony Robbins Companies in Europe, Fiji, Puerto Rico and the United States. In this program, featuring such influencers as Deepak Chopra and Caroline Myss, Loren has demonstrated the power of living in balance. Loren has a

---

passion for guiding people to live a completely balanced life in every aspect including health, finances, spirituality and relationships.

Loren also dedicates her life work to health and wellness. She currently holds the position of National Marketing Director for JuicePlus+, is a certified nutritional therapist and an accomplished speaker on various health related topics.

Loren firmly believes in helping all mankind and puts her beliefs into actions with her commitment to Las Vegas St Jude Youth Board, the Basket Brigade and many other organizations.

Drama Free Divorce Detox is Loren's third book. She also authored The Greatest Love; Being an extraordinary mom and Life Tune-ups; Your Personal Plan to Find Balance, Discover Your Passion and Step into Greatness. All her books are available at Amazon.com.

Introduction

If You Aren't In Control Of Your Life Then Who Is?

If you're going through hell, keep going.

—*Winston Churchill*

If you have picked up this book, odds are that you are in a difficult place in your life right now. You may be wondering if there will ever be more to your marriage. You may be in the middle of the brutal process of divorce (no matter how amicable, divorce is never easy). You may be newly divorced and struggling to drop your baggage in order to move forward. Whichever path you are on, I know one thing; it took a lot of hard work and difficult decision making to get to this point. It is never easy once you arrive at the realization that this relationship that once upon a time brought you so much joy is now toxic. Or when you came to the shocking realization that you have stopped being true to yourself; although you aren't quite sure exactly when that happened. Sometimes divorce is an eruption of negative events; often explosive and always painful. At other times it just creeps up silently and without notice until one day you look at your spouse and truthfully see how far apart you have drifted. In some cases, you know in your heart that divorce is the right thing to do. Sadly, in other cases, you aren't the one making the call. Right or not, it still hurts like hell.

Three Words That Will Pave Your Detox Path

Throughout the book and throughout your detox journey you will see a pattern of three simple words.

Rediscover

Reclaim

Reinvent

Each word represents a path and the combination of all three represents the new you that will emerge at the end of your detox.

You will start to see that there are many times in life when we need to stop and rediscover...reclaim...reinvent. This applies to our relationships of every kind: with ourselves, our spouse, our children, our parents, our siblings, our colleagues and with our faith. It goes without saying that as we experience life, we change. Some changes occur naturally when we grow as a person, some changes are prompted by our situation and some by our surroundings. Regardless of why we change, it will be a time of rediscovery, reclaiming and reinvention.

You will see those words repeatedly as you read Drama Free Divorce Detox. Let them resonate with you. It is important that they become part of your detox process.

What Exactly Is a Drama Free Divorce Detox?

What I mean when I say "Drama Free Divorce Detox," I mean ridding yourself of everything and anything that can and will block you from moving forward towards a happy and fulfilling life. Let's face it—divorce SUCKS! Even under the best of circumstance there are going to be raw emotions, negative build-up and hurt feelings in the process.

This book is NOT about bad-mouthing your ex, ripping pictures in half or throwing away all of the amazing memories of better times that you shared together; quite the opposite. It's about facing (not avoiding) the necessary emotions that surface during divorce. Hurt, shame, guilt, anger, resentment, grief, and denial are all part of the package. Detox is about giving yourself permission to release all that crap. It is about learning to replace the ugly parts of the marriage and divorce with the positive things that will feed your spirit and your soul. It is about reclaiming the real you!

Is now the right time?

I am often asked, "How do you know when it's time for a detox?" Four little words…. Listen to your gut. You will get that feeling; you know the one, when you feel deep down inside that something just isn't quite right. When you wake up one day and realize that the end is inevitable. Even under the worst circumstances, we often stay put because we feel that being in a bad marriage isn't as bad as being alone. I'm not going to lie, the unknown is damn scary. It is doubly scary if you have children to consider. No matter how hard you try to rationalize with yourself, your gut won't lie. You will know when it is time for a change. If you have read this far than chances are that you already know.

Why detox?

Any time we hear the word "detox" we immediately associate it with things like drug addiction, alcoholism or unhealthy eating. It has a negative stigma attached to it but in all actuality detox is a great thing. It means you have decided to make positive changes. You are choosing to purge yourself of the bad things in our life. Is detox hard? YES. Is it a bad thing? Absolutely not. How can taking back control of your life be a bad thing? Once you make it to the other side of any detox program, you begin to feel so much better. Drama Free Divorce Detox has the same benefits. That carton of ice cream, that pack of cigarettes, that displaced anger are all Band-Aids trying to hide what you are really going through emotionally and physically. By choosing to actively participate in your detox, you will rip off that Band-Aid and work your way through all the painful parts. The result will be a person who is healthy, rejuvenated, and ready to embrace the next phase of their life.

How did I get here?

It is very common to suddenly find yourself wondering how you got where you are now. Wondering, "Where did my life take this turn and how did I not see this coming?" We often feel blindsided. The first step to correcting that feeling is to look

---

inside and take an inventory. Grab a sheet of paper, take a deep breath and answer these 5 questions. Remember, there is no right or wrong answer….just honest ones. Write from the heart. If you feel like crap….write it down… pissed...write it down.

1. Where am I right now in this relationship?

2. What emotions am I feeling?

3. Where do I want to be?

4. What do I need to close the gap from where I am to where I want to be?

5. Do I have a support system to accompany me on this journey?

Hold on to your answers. Tuck them away somewhere. We will be revisiting these questions down the road.

While no two divorce situations are alike, I want you to know that I am speaking from experience. Been there…done that! I understand where you are right now. I want to use my experience to help you survive this difficult time and arrive at a place of healing and happiness as I have.

Being friends with your current spouse, soon to be ex-spouse or current ex-spouse is something that not only looks impossible to you at this point in time but actually may be something you have little or no interest in achieving. That is understandable. Why would you want a relationship with someone who you view to be a major contributor to the pain and unhappiness that you

---

are experiencing? I will tell you why. Once upon a time, a long long time ago, that person who you may despise right now had some amazing qualities that you fell in love with. I will show you how you can divorce, reclaim/rediscover/reinvent yourself and enjoy a great friendship with your ex.

In my case, I was the one who initiated the divorce. Asking the kids' dad for a divorce was the hardest thing I have ever done. Thankfully, over time, I have reached a place in my heart where I can finally feel gratitude for having met my husband and for all the amazing years we had together. I do not regret my marriage. At the risk of sounding cliché it helped me to grow into the woman that I am today. Not to mention that it gave me the greatest gifts in my life, my three beautiful children.

I met my husband Shore through the Basket Brigade; a wonderful program run by The Anthony Robbins Companies in which baskets of food are delivered to those in need on Thanksgiving. This experience of giving back inspired me at a time in my life when I was feeling a bit empty and dissatisfied. Shortly after this, I began to travel with Tony and his team which only strengthened my relationship with Shore. He was amazing and I loved learning from him. He was number one in sales, was a team-leader and a kick-ass speaker. I saw so many characteristics in him that I wanted to develop in myself; I felt so excited by the possibility of everything that we could create together both personally and professionally.

To be honest, although our relationship was based on a friendship like no other, something was lacking. I suppressed my desires for a different type of relationship because I really valued the fact that we were such great friends. That was a high priority for me. For so much of my life I felt like so many other women feel; that guys only wanted me for sex. It felt so good to finally have a relationship that was founded on something much deeper. I was not willing to risk that to try to change our relationship. I convinced myself that I could make it work. If anyone could it was me; after all, I worked in an industry of empowerment where there is a strong belief that you can make anything happen if you want it badly enough. And so we were married.

I turned to work as a way to fill the "something" I felt was missing. I put all my energy into my career and immersed myself in a ton of projects. At home, I did as so many wives do and I placed my husband in the role of "head of household" whether he wanted it or not. We both worked, traveled and parented but Shore was the family's primary decision maker and money manager. Twenty years passed and our "friendship" marriage was surviving. My first gut feeling came when a financial matter surfaced. As we know from statistics, the #1 thing married couples fight about is money. While Shore and I never really fought, I felt angry inside and had hit a pivotal point in our marriage.

As with many marriages we chose to be passive aggressive instead of really expressing our feelings. By sweeping these major issues under the rug we never resolved anything. This approach, while easier, caused my inner negativity to fester. I wanted so badly to scream, let the flood gates open and get it all out on the table but I wanted to be loved more than I wanted to be right. I just knew that nobody would love me the way he loved me.

The thing to remember is that sacrificing the "true" you comes at a very high price. You begin to feel sick physically and emotionally. It may take a while for you to even notice things are slowly creeping in and causing you to be unhappy. Often when we experience bad vibes we find it easier to swat them away like an annoying gnat instead of facing the truth. Choosing instead to believe that one day things will get better.

While I would describe my relationship with Shore as happy it had also become toxic in many ways. Crucial things were missing. We no longer had meals together as a family which was something we both loved doing. It honestly felt as if our lives were running on parallel paths. I knew in my heart that things just weren't right.

I will always remember "The Day" . . . the day I made the decision that I needed a serious detox. I was lying in bed in our beautiful home watching CSI. Shore was trying to launch a new business and spent most of his time in our home office. I felt as if he was never around anymore. Emotionally I was lonely and angry and I channeled those emotions into watching a show about anger. Imagine that, I work in personal development yet I was watching a show that was the exact opposite of everything I believed. I realized that I was losing my sense of purpose.

How the hell could I be losing my sense of purpose??? I was on a total winning streak in my professional life. My book, Life Tuneups, was in People magazine. Through my company, Lobella, I was involved in our empowering women's groups. I had speaking engagements at spas throughout the country. My direct sales business, Juice Plus, was soaring beyond belief. Despite all of these positive milestones I was still lonely, sad and lacking purpose. And right there and then, watching CSI, I had an epiphany.

"Hold on just a damn minute! Who IS this person? Why am I watching shows about people being murdered? This is NOT me! I want the old "me" back. The fun "me"! The "me" who loves reading great books and posting inspirational quotes."

Without knowing why or how, I knew that I had lost those things that were important to me. I had let this unhealthy relationship mainline negativity and distraction into my life. I was becoming sick and I could not, would not go on feeling this way any longer. I knew it was time to change! Not just for me but for Shore and our children.

Be Prepared

I was inspired to write this book because while you may not know where the path ahead will lead, I want you to be prepared. As much as you'd like to, you can't skip certain emotions along the way. You can't skip the anger! You can't skip the frustration! You can't skip the sadness! You need to acknowledge and embrace all the crap that you are going to go through. During detox you need to experience all the ugly parts before you can reach that place where you feel revitalized and renewed.

Commit to following through for yourself, your health, your sanity, your relationship and your family. Be smart when preparing for this detox. I bet that right now you are saying, "What have I gotten myself into? Do I really want to go through with this?" My answer to you is a resounding, "YES!" In order to move forward, you have to resolve to let go of the past. As The Anthony Robbins Companies says, "You can't move forward using the rear view mirror as your guide." Prepare your mind and your heart for this experience. Embrace the fact (as scary as it seems) that you are going to let go of certain things. You may have no idea what they are right now but they will present themselves throughout the process. Just remember that release is good!

If you really allow yourself to feel every feeling, every experience and every step of Drama Free Divorce Detox, you will ultimately feel at peace with your decision. You will find your way back to your true self who will be even more fabulous than before. Are you ready to be the person who knows what they need and isn't afraid to ask for it? The person who knows they deserve the kind of love they always imagined? Well, get ready because here it comes.

I want to end by congratulating you. I hope that by taking this first step you are seeing just how strong and amazing you are. Baby steps are still steps in the right direction. I am proud of you and you should be very proud of yourself. My wish for you is to minimize the heartache and the growing pains. This is your guide should you choose to accept your life mission and facilitate the process. So let's have some fun together, starting out by acknowledging how much you've accomplished in life so far.

Take my hand, and let's go on this adventure together. The yellow brick road actually does lead to a life of fulfillment and joy. Like Dorothy in the Wizard of Oz, all you need is already inside you. It's time for you to Rediscover, Reclaim, and Reinvent the true You!

Shore and I are living proof that you can take a toxic marriage and turn it into a successful divorce. You are courageously taking the path to a healthier you and to maintaining a "friendship" status with the person who you saw many great things in so many years ago.

Let the journey begin!

It is time to fill your baggage with the things you will need to fully engage in the detox process. Trust me on the items…they will make perfect sense once we get started.

Faith

Open mind

A journal and pen

Tissues

A great support group

Lots of patience

Photos of great moments with your ex

Supplies to create a vision board (check out my Pinterest page for ideas)

Book Tips: As you go through this book you will see these three (3) icons:

In certain chapters, I will share how that topic applied to my personal situation. I have opened up my heart and soul. All of my stories are real, raw and honest.

Many chapters will have a "to-do" exercise noted by this icon. I highly suggest that you stop and complete the "to-do" before moving onto the next chapter. The exercises play a key role in rediscovering, reclaiming and reinventing yourself.

Time to Get Juiced: Juice is known to have a positive effect on our health as well as our emotions and mental clarity. Certain chapters will have juice recipes that are signified by this icon. I encourage you to give the recipes a try. This book will also serve a great resource long after you have read it for the first time.

WARNING!
DANGER
ZONE

Detox is not a time to sugar coat things or sweep them under the rug. It is a time for brutal honestly that will allow you to move forward positively and confidently. No more second guessing. That is why you will find that I tell it like it is.

This book is not for the timid. Some of the language may be offensive. Some of the content will take you to the place where the "raw" stuff lives and that is never fun.

You may end up divorcing more than just your spouse. You may also learn that you also need to divorce some of your beliefs, ideals and rules that you have held fast to for way too long.

The good news is that by giving yourself permission to explore the rawness, allowing the pain, divorcing everything that is no longer healthy for you and encouraging healing, you open yourself up to a brand new life where you are free to marry much better beliefs, ideas and rules.

I promise you that if you follow the book through your detox process the end result will be nothing short of AWESOME!

Part One

Stop The
Crazy Train!
Get On Track
To
A Fulfilling
Life !

She will not be able to fulfill her function if she remains with a man who derides her glory.

—Marianne Williamson

I am so glad you are here. By turning the page it can only mean one thing; something resonated deep within and you are ready to get started on your journey to healing and becoming whole again! Before we start I want you to know that you are not alone. Besides having a support group of friends and family who love you, you also have Drama Free Divorce Detox family. I would encourage you to join our Facebook group now. It will be another great resource for you at all stages of your detox and far afterwards. I look forward to chatting with you at Drama Free Divorce Detox (Facebook - https://www.facebook.com/dramafreedivorcedetox and Twitter at @nodramadivorce).

Now, let's get to it.

Chapter 1 :

One...Two...Three Types of Relationships

Before we start, we need to take a look at relationships. Essentially, there are only three (3) types of relationships:

- Relationship with ourselves

- Relationship with others

- Relationship with whatever high power we believe in

If asked to put them in order of importance, how would you rank them? Sadly, many people put "relationship with self" at the bottom of the pecking order. I am no exception! One quote that now has new relevance for me is:

He who knows others is wise.

He who knows himself is enlightened.

-Lao Tzu

The person who really helped me through "the toughest decision of my life," is my friend, Jamie Greene. I was at my wits end. I had freaking tried EVERYTHING to help get solutions to my problems. Then one day, just like in the movie Bruce Almighty when he says, "Just show me a sign!" I got a sign. That sign came in the form of a Facebook post from Jamie, a Psychotherapist and "Unconventional" Coach.

I really needed his help and didn't have the money to do sessions with him but in the words of The Anthony Robbins Companies: "If you can't, you must."

Jamie helped me to open up and ask the questions that I needed to ask. As hard as it was, Shore and I did sessions together. At times I honestly felt as if I was losing it. I couldn't even identify myself. We both wanted (and needed) to be whole again.

One of the greatest lessons I learned from Jamie is that there is no substitute for the relationship with oneself. Let me repeat that… there is no substitute for the relationship with oneself. I had an identity about myself that I thought was pretty clear. I was wrong. Obviously, there was something that wasn't fulfilling otherwise I wouldn't have felt so lost in my relationship with others. I have always been very driven and never realized the pressure I was putting on myself and others. I wanted others to be proud of me. I wanted them to know I would just go for it, whatever it took.

Jamie suggests that people ask themselves this key question in order to identify what is going on in their lives, "What

are the barriers that are keeping me from my true self...
authentically...without judgment?"

We often try to protect ourselves by raising defense
mechanisms. Defense is used to protect us from pain and
abuse. We go into a trance, create barriers, build walls, shut
down and close our heart.

Jamie helped me to discover and understand the different
ways to protect myself; consciously or subconsciously. Is it
serving you, or not serving you? If you are willing to explore the
cause and be open, you can learn. Shift your thinking so it
becomes an adventure as opposed to depressing.

In order to move in the direction of resolution, a supportive
environment is needed. It is key to recognize the importance of
community and support. With the breakdown of self-worth, it's
vital to love ourselves and allow ourselves to receive. What we
need are role models, mentors, a place where we can feel
respected and safe. Jamie kept me to my higher standard and
on target to remain consistent.

Was it hard? Horribly hard...

Was it worth it? Yes.

Was it a stretch? Yes.

It is critical that you look at things in your life the way Jamie
made me look at mine. Look at what your "must nevers" are for
yourself. What are the "musts?" Look at your "should" and

"should nots." ONLY then can you address what you need from others.

I learned that I could not expect things from others if I wasn't living it myself? I realized that I needed to really get to know me and renew the me that I KNEW was waiting to emerge!

What I appreciated the most about my relationship with Jamie is that I knew he would be honest with me. To tell me things that would stir me, no matter how painful it might be.

If you are one of the many who want to place "relationship with self" in the last slot of importance, now is the time to change that mindset. Your relationship with yourself must take priority over your relationship with others. If you focus on yourself, your mental and physical health, only then can you nurture healthy relationships with others.

As for me, I started to tone up. I changed my psychology about food and about my physical outcomes. I knew I had to return to the discipline that once drove me before I became toxic. I began to change my Identity to reflect my new journey. With Jamie's help I knew one thing for sure, "I'm gonna be okay."

 I want you to spend some time in reflection. Think about the three types of relationships: Self, Others and Higher Being. Where do you honestly rank "self?" How does putting others before yourself affect your relationship?

I will say it over and over, there are no wrong answers. Reflect with honesty. This exercise is the first step to shifting your

---

mindset. You are no longer in last place! Love yourself. Respect yourself!

In the Words of Aristotle:

When talking about relationships with others, we cannot overlook the words of the Greek philosopher Aristotle. He noted that there are three kinds of relationships (friendships) that we can have with others. However, it was Aristotle's belief that only one could bring true happiness.

o   Relationships of Pleasure

o   Relationship of Utility

o   Relationship of Shared Virtue

While I should not dare paraphrase the great Philosopher, I'm going to anyway.

Relationship of Pleasure is probably very self-explanatory. The term booty call comes to mind. Not necessarily a bad thing if both people are looking for a pleasurable companionship without deep connection or commitment.

Relationship of Utility reminds me of a business transaction. You buy your meat from a butcher. You get the meat you want and he gets money. A win win. In relationships, this may look like a trophy wife scenario or a marriage of "show" for whatever reason. Everyone gets what they want however there is no real relationship; no genuine love connection.

A Relationship of Shared Virtue, well just the name alone makes it sound awesome. It is also self-explanatory. When we think of "virtue" we think of a quality in someone that inherently makes them morally good. Being in a relationship with a partner who is morally good automatically gives them a checkmark in the "I can trust you" category. It also allows us to feel certain that they are out to make the world, their personal world and the global world, a better place.

It is no surprise that sometimes we marry our relationship of pleasure, our relationship of utility or our relationship of shared virtue and it simply doesn't work out. Regardless of what type of relationship it was or who called it quits, the emotions begin a roller coaster ride that is often too wild a ride to bear.

Chapter 2:

What the Hell is Normal?

The question that I'm asked most often is "Am I supposed to be feeling this way?" If you are feeling it then you are supposed to be feeling it. There is no cookie cutter checklist of post-divorce feelings. All situations are different and all people are unique in the way they handle certain circumstances. Your emotions are taking you down a path that needs to be identified, explored and conquered before you can move on. One thing is certain; it is not a quick fix.

When we are affected by a death of a loved one or friend, it is expected that we will go through a mourning period. This period consists of us working through the 7 Steps of Grief. However, those steps are not exclusive to death in the physical sense. The grief process applies to any event that creates a "death" of your reality the way you know it. Cancer patients, upon receiving their diagnosis, will often go through a grief process. A "death" of sorts has come to the life they had dreamed of living. According to support groups for gay/lesbian/bisexual/transgendered, once a child comes out to their family it is common for the parents to go through a grieving process. The "death" has come to the life they have envisioned for their son or daughter since the day they were born. Divorce is a "death" as well. It is a death of our "happily ever after," or our dreams of how we would retired and spend our golden years with the person we married.

Here is a glimpse of the 7 Steps of Grief (adapted towards divorce) which may help answer the question of "Am I supposed to be feeling this way."

1. **Shock & Denial:** Regardless of who initiated the discussion of divorce the chances are high that your reaction was one of numbed disbelief. By being at a stage of shock and denial, you isolate yourself for what is about to come. During this time it is not uncommon to continue to believe the marriage will last or to actively pursue your spouse (even if he or she has moved on).

2. **Pain & Guilt:** Shock and denial will be replaced with unbelievable pain as well as guilt. This is the stage where you may begin to wonder what you could have done differently. You may feel remorse over things that were (or were not) said and things that you did (or didn't) do. Many people have a hard time tolerating this stage of grief however it is very important that you do not move

on until you have fully experienced the pain and not just put a Band-Aid on it. A word of caution: This is also the stage where people often seek an escape through drugs or alcohol.

3. **Anger:** Pain, guilt and remorse are often followed by anger and bargaining. You will want to place blame and lash out in anger. It is important to use caution as it is way too easy to say something out of anger that you will regret later.

4. **Bargaining:** With anger comes bargaining with our higher power. It is not uncommon to deal with divorce by offering up a bargain in hopes of making things better. "I will stop/start doing XYZ if you will just let him or her do blah blah blah."

5. **Depression and Reflection:** This is one stage where your friends and family may accuse you of "wallowing" but this stage is just as important as any other. Reality has set in about the true magnitude of the situation. You need time to process everything that has happened. This is the time where it is important that you choose to focus on the good times. While there will still be some anger and frustration, this time of reflection is what will allow you to come out with a decent (if not wonderful) relationship with your ex.

6. **Reconstruction:** Aahhhh…. A light at the end of the dark dark tunnel. In this stage you will begin can see it and will start adjusting to your new independent life.

Depression starts to lift and you will feel calmer and more in control. Your mind will actually begin to feel as if it is fully functional again. You will see the problems that arose from the situation more clearly and begin to solve them with practical solutions and not with hasty emotion. It is a time for recreating "you" as an individual and not as part of a couple.

7. **Acceptance:** This final stage of grief allows you to accept your situation (doesn't mean you have to be happy about it). You will look forward to the future and what amazing things it holds in store. You are able to think about your ex without the agonizing anger, sadness or pain.

It is very important that you know that even though there are 7 steps it does not mean that the grieving process is a structured process. For some people it may naturally go from 1 to 2 to 3 … and with each step they begin to feel stronger but for others it is not going to be that organized. Grief tends to sway like the breeze. You may have three great days in a row and then be blindsided with a day of depression that you can hardly bear. There is also no assigned time frame. With each divorce situation being different it only makes sense that the time frame would fluctuate from circumstance to circumstance. If you were in shock over the news that your spouse was leaving you and had been having an affair, it stands to reason that you may spend more time in the "shock" phase or the "anger" phase. If the divorced is amicable you may spend very little time in those phases.

I wanted to touch on the steps of grief to show you that any of those stages, any combination of those stages are all perfectly normal reactions to divorce. Keep in mind that grieving is a very personal process. Do not let others rush you. Take your time in dealing with your loss now and you will find that the pain doesn't keep resurfacing though the years; derailing your happiness in the future.

I honestly didn't think I needed any help but the truth is that I was drowning. Once I admitted that I was fooling myself, I tried to put up a strong front to show that I could get through this on my own. I had successfully tackled anything else in my life that was a challenge so why should this be any different. And not to mention, I was the one who asked for the divorce. If I made that decision shouldn't it be easier for me than if he had asked for the divorce? This attitude fooled those around me who could've helped had I simply reached out to them. I didn't. So people naturally thought "Oh, she's strong. I've seen her make it through worse crap before." "For God sake she works with The Anthony Robbins Companies – the epitome of strength and empowerment, she'll be just fine." But I wasn't fine by any stretch of the imagination. I was quickly losing myself. I couldn't handle it.

Pear-fectly Delicious

- 2 – celery stalks
- 2 - pears
- ½ - small cabbage
- Watercress (handful)

Wash all ingredients and juice. Serve over ice. This recipe is for liver health and is rich in calcium, potassium, magnesium and vitamins A, C, and K.

Chapter 3:

A Damn Tough Decision to Make

Let's face it – when it comes to divorce someone has to be the one to make the decision to say the "D" word for the first time. For some of you, the decision to divorce was made for you. For others, you have already made the decision, shared your decision with your spouse and are beginning (or have completed) the divorce process. If you fall into those two categories please do not skip this section. Reflecting on why and how the divorce decision was made is part of the detox process.

Now, for those of you who are in the process of making the divorce decision definitely do not skip this section. The process of battling your emotions, feeling guilty over even having the thought of divorce, weighing the pros and cons, losing sleep due to mentally playing his reaction in your head over and over are all a part of the decision making process.

To Do: Start by taking some time to jot down these questions, reflect on them and write your thoughts. I say "some time" but I really mean take as much time as you need. This may take you 30 minutes over a cup of coffee or you may want to think about it for days in order to give yourself the real and true answers that you are seeking. Keep in mind that by glossing over, blocking out or sugar coating you are only hurting your recovery process. No one will see this but you so let it out.

- Are my spouse and I heading in the same direction?

- Were we heading in the same direction a year ago?

- Are our values and priorities the same?

- Were our values and priorities the same a year ago?

- Are we still growing together?

- Is "growing apart" a more accurate assessment?

- Do we communicate well?

- Did we communicate well a year ago?

- Do you feel as if something crucial is missing in your marriage?

- Do you feel that something crucial is missing within you personally?

- What was the turning point in our relationship?

If I had to bet, I would say that you got half way through that writing assignment and had a strong feeling (one way or the other) about your decision. Did reflecting on those questions confirm what your gut has been telling you? Is something just not quite right? Have you been denying the poisonous parts of your relationship to avoid seeing the truth?

While there is no "one size fits all" pre-screening exercise on what to look for when things are going astray in a marriage, there are facts. Plain and simple (well maybe not so simple).

As you are going through your detox process is it very important to try to identify the turning point. Be honest about what occurred that started to drive the wedge between you and your spouse. Many times we don't want to look at the cause because it is hard to grasp. One of the most trying times in a marriage is also one of the most beautiful, the birth of a baby. Sometimes the loss of a job, death of a loved one or change in finances cause so much stress that the couple just can't regroup and recover.

No two marriages are the same but many couples have things they would consider "deal breakers" in a marriage which will cause the union to end in divorce. Among the most common deal breakers are:

- Dishonesty
- Change in priorities
- Cheating
- Abuse
- Addiction

A new study conducted by researchers at Kansas State University surveyed 4,500 couples on the topic of arguments. Fights over finances are a main factor in divorce regardless of the couple's income level. The study also concluded that during financial fights the couples used harsher language, the fights lasted longer and recovery period post financial fight is longer.

During your exploration you may find that there was not just one turning point. There may have been something that was red flag, followed by another red flag and then finally the straw that broke the camel's back. Often the straw can be something small but following red flag after red flag, it quickly becomes the breaking point.

In the introduction I mentioned the first red flag when my husband and I were trying to work through a financial situation. The second turning point occurred when I was getting ready to do an event in Australia. I was folding laundry and packing my bag together for the trip when Shore said, "I support my wife. I support my wife. I support wife" with a bit of a snarky attitude.

While the words themselves may have seemed nice; the tone was anything but. There was no pride in his voice, in fact he sounded a little bit angry, the way guys get when something doesn't go their way. My heart sank. More than anything, I wanted my man to be proud of me. I thought that he wanted me to accomplish great things. I was going to achieve great things for our family.

It was this second red flagged that caused the new "me-in-waiting" to begin to emerge. She raised an eyebrow and said with full truth what I was thinking at that very moment... something the old me would never have said.

Unwavering I said, "You're jealous,"

"No I'm not," was his reply of denial.

With all my courage I insisted, "Yes, you are."

And then the truth came out.... the real underlying issue....."Well, you get to do your things, and I'm still trying to do my own stuff. . . ."

It was at that exact moment when I felt our relationship shift. My husband so badly wanted his own business ventures to work out. He wanted to step up yet nothing seemed to be coming to fruition.

Shortly after this exchange my family joined me as I gave a presentation to an audience of over 7000 people. The presentation went well and my message was openly received. Afterwards my husband, our daughter and I posed for a photo. The saying, "A picture is worth 1000 words" could not have been truer on that day. His expression, as he looked over at me was not even close to convey the message of "I support my wife." His expression was clearly "When is it going to be my time."

This single picture confirmed that it was time. There was no quick fix for how toxic our relationship had become. If I was going to salvage the friendship I needed to make this critical decision and get the process started.

Chapter 4:

He Feels/She Feels

Once you have made the decision or once you have been told of your spouse's wishes for a divorce, there are three common reactions: the earthquake, the heartbreak, or the handshake. Most people will experience one of these three. Can you recognize your own reaction or the reaction of your spouse in one of these?

Three Types of Divorce

This is where the fun begins. You start to get rid of the relationships, including perhaps your romantic or intimate relationship. To help you identify the relationship you are in, here are three types of divorce along with the identifying factors.

The Earthquake: When one spouse suddenly decides to leave the relationship with no prior warning, it can feel like the ground has literally shifted below your feet. In this situation, your spouse may essentially say, "I'm out of here." Often this feels as if it's out of the blue and you are stunned because you thought everything was fine in your relationship. This can be especially painful because you didn't see it coming. You are shocked at yourself and how you could have been so out of touch with their feelings. Do not blame yourself. In an earthquake divorce, one spouse is generally very good at hiding his or her feelings. Sometimes the spouse will know exactly why they want to leave (such as an affair) or sometimes they may just know they need to go but can't really communicate it (such as a mid-life crisis).

Once you catch your breath, the next step is to climb out of the cracks, brush the dust off, get back on your feet, seek guidance, get assertive and move forward.

5 Identifying Factors:

o   Sudden and Unexpected

o   Feeling of Turbulence

o   Feeling Unprepared

o   Feeling Shock

o   Feeling Fear

The Heartbreak – When one spouse shares that they simply can't go on any longer in the relationship, it's a heartbreak divorce. You don't want a divorce. It tugs at your heart and may leave you feeling completely hollow. Usually this either stems from a reason such as one of the spouses having a shift in priorities, a spouse is not feeling appreciated or one person no longer has feeling for the other; simply put they have fallen out of

---

love. It may be due to a particular situation that the couple has been trying to work through but the relationship is simply beyond repair. Unlike the "earthquake", the "heartbreak" is generally less shocking and there tend to be more warning signs.

With great effort, you move forward in a cloudy, lethargic coma. Any path of healing needs a support system but when you are experiencing heartache, you are also going to need that shoulder to cry on; someone to reassure you that "life is not over" and to join you in the occasional glass of wine.

This can serve as one of the most troubling experiences but can also give you an opportunity to begin creating a new you. Your heart might be broken but now you get to piece it back together with your choice of glue.

Five identifying factors of heartbreak:

o   Dishonesty

o   Lack of trust

o   Uncertainty

o   Abandonment

o   Loss of respect for each other

The Handshake – Once upon a time, you and your 'better half' saw the stars in each other's eyes. Now you find yourself balancing your checkbook. What you had just isn't there anymore. The "handshake" occurs when both parties mutually recognize that the relationship is over. Some view this as the best case scenario. While it might be less hostile it is still going to be extremely difficult. The grieving process will still occur. There is still the uneasy task of including lawyers (an unfortunate must), decisions to make regarding kids, property and finances. Luckily, you and your partner have managed to come to an amicable agreement that benefits each of you. Your friendship is easily salvageable based on the fact that you both agree on the marriage coming to a close. You wish each other well.

Even though this sounds like the best divorce scenario, you may still mourn the end of a chapter in your life and it's important to work through the steps instead of ignoring your feelings. Honor those emotions and take the time to detox so you can move on to a healthier, happier, new phase in your life.

Jamie and his (ex) wife are the perfect example of this type of divorce. It wasn't easy but they showed how divorce could be done with mutual respect and care. Divorce in a noble way. It not only showed a couple divorcing in a different way but it gave other people encouragement that they could do the same.

Five identifying factors of the Handshake:

o   Mutual agreement to part ways

o   The feeling "just isn't there" anymore

o   You maintain respect for each other

o   It's an easier transition from marriage

o   You're both capable of being civil

Regardless of which type of reaction you experience, your ultimate goal should be to return to:

The Keepsake. This will allow you to feel gratitude for all that you learned from this marriage and have a healthy, respectful relationship with your ex. This is healthy for both you and your husband but it is an absolute MUST if you have children together. Drama Free Divorce Detox will help you to reach this place of acceptance, forgiveness, and appreciation for the love you once felt.

Chapter 5

Stop... Not slow down...Not Speed up... STOP!

This is the shortest chapter in the book. The whole chapter is just expanding on one word: STOP

- **Stop** the excuses for why you're not going after your dreams.

- **Stop** justifying your actions and make decisions with conviction.

- **Stop** shrinking, playing small and trying to be invisible.

- **Stop** hanging around people who aren't helping you grow to be your best.

- **Stop** letting those poisonous thoughts enter your mind.

- **Stop** being emotionally constipated.

- **Stop** living in fear.

- **Stop** comparing yourself.

- **Stop** using the food, thoughts, alcohol and drugs that push down your true self.

- **Stop** compromising what you say or do because you think you'll lose a friendship or intimate relationship with your honesty.

There you have it! And if saying it once would make it all just stop than this would be the last chapter as well as the shortest. Unfortunately for us, saying it doesn't automatically make it so. What it does make it is a goal. A goal of exploring where you have been and a goal of rediscovery!

So, STOP! Make a cup of your favorite tea (for me, it was Southern sweet tea; a little something yum and sugary from my past) and grab your journal. Take a few minutes and think about some story/stories you have been telling yourself. A story that you bought into and have been living all these years. Why are you trapped in that story? What is it that has been holding you back from moving forward? What are the emotions that have been debilitating you? What are the actions that have inhibited your personal growth? What are the excuses that you have been making? Do you think others believe your story? Do you have them fooled or are you only fooling yourself?

And then decide...what can you begin to do that will allow yourself to STOP living in that story. What can you do to free

---

yourself and to begin to build your new true reality. Write down whatever comes to mind. There does not need to be a rhyme or reason to your writing. Just get it out of your head and onto your paper. As you move along in your journey the words you write today will all start to become perfectly clear.

Red Deliciousness

- 2 – medium apples

- 5 - carrots

- 1 – lemon (peeled)

- ½ c- dandelion greens

- 1 oz. - fresh beet

Wash all ingredients and juice. Serve over ice. This recipe is a great liver detox and is rich in antioxidants, calcium, iron and vitamins A, B, C, E and K

Chapter 6:

Own It.

Making the decision may be hard but questioning your decision days, weeks, months or even years later will absolutely kill your spirit. It is critical that the moment you make the decision that you own it. Everyone from your spouse, your mother, your best friend to your boss will inevitably ask you "are you sure" and your answer should always be an unwavering "yes". You can follow that "yes" with a supporting statement such as "trust me, I've given this more thought that you can ever imagine."

No matter how confident you say it, there will always be a few people who start out as non-supporters. It can feel very disheartening and add more stress to an already extremely stressful time in your life. Sometimes it is very hard to understand why people just can't be supportive.

Remember when you were a kid, wide eyed and curious about the world around you. You dreamed of being a ballerina, pro football star, a princess or the president. Most likely your parents told you that you could be anything in the world you wanted to be. When you faced difficult times (in the eyes of a child) like learning to ride a bike or making friends at a new school, you knew you could always count on your support system to be on your side. Yet when we become adults, the decisions that we make for our lives are often met with criticism.

Wouldn't it be magnificent if the people closest to you in your life would always be your biggest cheerleaders? All too often our well-intentioned friends and family can deflate our confidence with their constant questioning and unwanted comments.

Let's focus on them for a minute. When it comes to the people in your life you need to really try to consider their point of view and where they are coming from when they offer their advice (solicited or unsolicited). Sometimes, while their words are directed at you and your situation, it may actually have more to do with them than you.

Consider this…

Is it possible that they are in just as much shock as you are about the decision you have made? After all, you have had time to get used to the idea but they are hearing it for the first time. Many friends and family do not immediately offer condolences for the loss of your marriage. They often choose to bombard you with a million and one questions about why, how did he or she take it, who is staying in the house and who gets the dog. They do not mean to be insensitive they are just trying to wrap their heads around the situation. However, while they are busy peppering us with questions, all we really want is a hug and a show of support.

Is it possible that they simply do not understand what you really want in life or who you are trying to become? After all, for as long as you have been married they thought that was what you wanted in life. You have changed the game plan and they no longer feel informed. When people do not understand something it is usually easier for them to approach the topic from a place of dislike as opposed to a place of support.

Is it possible that they are concerned that your decision will take you on a path or change you so much that they will no longer have a place in your life? Your desire to grow, forge forward, become independent may appear to them that you are moving ahead in a life that may or may not include them.

Although it is hard to not to take it personally, people tend to process everything from a "me" stand point first. Who knows, maybe your brevity and determination is something they have considered and were never strong enough to act upon. You really never know what people are going through and you will be surprised what people tell you once you proclaim your decision.

Some people, although poor communicators really will be interested in your situation and the new path you want to walk down. Share with them openly and honestly. No, you do not have to share all the gory details of you marriage but you can be open about your struggles. Always let them know that you are thankful for their support. If they do not seem to understand or agree, do not try to sell them on the idea. You do not have to air all the dirty laundry in order to convince them. It is best to just speak confidently that this is what is best in your life at this point in time. With a clearer understanding of where your head and heart are they are sure to come around and will begin to be your cheerleader again.

What about people who are relentless? No matter how hard you try they will never see your point of view. They have already made up their mind and there is little you can do to convince them otherwise. This reaction can be very discouraging, frustrating & disheartening. Know that you cannot control the actions of others. Once you learn that lesson you will be much happier.

In those cases your communication skills are going to have to come into play. When you are firm and confident in your words you will send the message that you do not feel the need to defend yourself or your choices. The best way to stop a barrage of questions or comments in their tracks is to be prepared with a simple statement such as "This is what is best for me and I am eager to move forward."

When they respond to that with another comment or question do not take the bait. Let them finish and reply with something such as "I understand that you are concerned however this is what is best for me and I'm eager to move forward".

By acknowledging that you heard them (not blocking out their words) and repeating your original statement you are showing them that you own your decision.

Sometimes a loved one simply cannot muster up supportive when you need it most which can be very hurtful. Try hard to let them know that you need them now more than ever. Communicating to them in a calm (not emotion charged) tone and saying "I love you and would really appreciate it if you could support me in this. It is something that I must do. I know you don't fully understand why I want to do it but I hope that you will trust me and support me in my journey" is sure to have an impact.

There is no doubt that you will need a support team no matter how small. If some people just don't come around right away, give them time. You have enough on your plate with your decision and detox. Do not add the additional stress of trying to convince others that you know what is best for you. It is your life, you have made your decision and you need to begin the healing process with or without them.

Chapter 7:

Six Divorces??? WTF!

As if one divorce isn't bad enough, there is a fascinating paper out of Oklahoma State University written by Mary K.

Lawler, RN, PH.D. Family Development Specialist. Entitled, Transitioning through Divorce: The Six Types of Divorce, the concept is that each divorce can potentially consist of six components. While this makes divorce sound even more overwhelming than it already is if you break the divorce process into individual sections it actually becomes more manageable and less muddied.

Dr. Lawler states that her Transitioning Through Divorce series is, "not intended to encourage divorce but to help individuals who have made that choice to have a 'good divorce'— where you maintain at least the same level of emotional well-being as before the divorce." This is very complimentary to Drama Free Divorce Detox theory which is why I felt it important to include her research.

The six types of divorce include:

1. Emotional

2. Legal

3. Economic

4. Co-parental

5. Community

6. Psychological

Emotional divorce can happen for years before the decision to pursue a legal divorce begins.

The legal divorce is the process of ending the relationship in the courts usually with the assistance of mediators and attorneys.

The economic divorce involves the task of dividing up property as well as finances.

The co-parental divorce is the negotiation that revolves around parental custody and responsibilities involving the children. It is crucial that during this time the child/children are spared from witnessing or overhearing any conflicts between parents. They must be reassured that while the adults will no longer be spouses, their role of parent is still very much intact.

The community divorce is how the end of the marriage is going to affect other relationships; your spouse's family members who you now consider your family, mutual friends, shared places such as the gym or place of worship.

The psychological divorce is part of the moving on process. It is learning to adapt to your new independence, learning new ways to communicate with your ex, no longer stalking their Facebook page and becoming okay with the fact that both of you are going to move on.

Now that you have read it can you see why I felt it was so important to share? By approaching each divorce segment separately you will be much more eloquent in your communication about that area. You will be clear about your thoughts if you stick to that topic and not continually bounce back and forth. Bouncing only blurs lines and makes for irrational thinking. If you are discussing property with your spouse or attorney, by focusing only on that portion of the divorce you will be much more successful in settling unfinished business.

Rainbow Rave

- 1 – beet, large (or 2-3 small)

- 3 – carambola (aka Star Fruit)

- ½ - pineapple

- 4 - oranges (peeled)

Wash all ingredients and juice. Serve over ice. Sit back and try to think of what candy this reminds you of. ☺ Hint: Taste the Rainbow

Part Two

Stay Healthy.
Release the S#&T

Sometimes when things are falling apart, they may actually be falling into place.

~Anonymous

In this section we are going to explore areas that will allow you be begin to move forward. You will take a look at the way you currently deal with life, where you are in different aspects of your life and begin to take back control of your life.

Chapter 8:

How You Do Anything is How You Do Everything

It is often said that how you play a game is how you show up in life. This is a very interesting concept.

TO DO

Forget about life for a second. I want you to just think about games. Maybe you played sports in school, played board games, any type of card games, games of chance or maybe you simply enjoy puzzles. Spend some time reflecting on how you approach games. Are you more comfortable being an observer or do you prefer to be team captain? What emotions do games stir in you? Do you want to win win win or would you throw a game to allow someone else to have the feeling of victory? Are you happy with the way you handle playing games?

As you were doing that exercise, could you begin to see a parallel of how you approach games and how you approach life? As with everything else in your detox, there is not a right or wrong answer. What these exercises do is to help you learn more about yourself.

You may have discovered that when it comes to games you:

- Follow the rules without exception

- You will sit out so others can play

- You are very competitive so losing is not an option

- Cheap shots are okay as long as you win

- It is all about having fun

If we apply these to your life it may look something like this:

Without rules there would be chaos. While this is a true statement doesn't it mean that you may be missing out on living your life to its fullest? Of course we should go to work every day and our children should go to school every day however isn't it fun to break those rules every once in a while? Playing hooky with your kids is great for mind, body and spirit. If you feel guilty about it then make part of your day educational by visiting a museum or hitting up the local library.

Everyone should have a turn. While is it nice to sit out so others can "play" it is not a very healthy approach. Example: You have scheduled to go to the gym at 5pm tonight but your mom calls at 4 and gives you a guilt trip about not making time for her. She asks if you can meet her for an early dinner at 5pm. Oh great! What to do? Well, everyone needs a turn and so everyone should get a turn. Learn to perfect your compromising skills. You also need to perfect your communications skills because as the saying goes you catch more flies with honey. A solution looks like this, "Mom, you are so right and I have missed seeing you. Unfortunately I cannot possibly do today at 5. I heard of a little place in town with a great brunch. Are you free Sunday at noon?" See what I did there? Everyone plays! You have validated her feelings while standing firm in your decision and offering a great compromise.

Losing is not an option. I get it, no one likes to lose or be considered a loser. You just need to always consider "at what cost." Pick your battles. We have heard that you may not win the battle but you can win the war. Often we need stop focusing on the immediate situation at hand and look at the big picture. Let's say you have a teenager. We all know what a challenge that can be. And let's say that your teen is terrible at doing homework, stays on his phone or computer until all hours of the night, insists on wearing jeans to a nice dinner out and thinks that the latest rapper is a god. If you try to change/correct each one of the "battles" you will end up losing all of them. Homework and a good night's sleep are very important as they affect their education (future) and their health (now). Set rules regarding homework and make electronics off limits after a certain hour. Jeans to dinner—while it is not what you would prefer it is not a battle to fight. Nor is their music selection. Should you choose to battle those two topics you run the risk of losing the other more important battles. This approach applies to children, coworkers, parents and friends. Losing is an option and a damn good one at times.

Hitting below the belt is acceptable. NEVER! In games as in life, when we feel that our backs are against the wall it is time to pull out the big guns (so to speak). As you watch professional basketball, football or baseball you often notice that everyone plays nice for the most part until the last few minutes in a close scoring game. While the clock is ticking, it is often in those last minutes that the players begin to try to get away with a few cheap shots. They have to do something to win the game and at this point playing fair will no longer work. How often have you found yourself losing an argument and you feel the clock is ticking. So you decide to use the cheap shot. You say something that attacks the other person's character not their actions or you dig up something from the past. This is certain to cause emotional pain to others and that is never okay.

It is all about having fun. Fun is a good thing. Everyone likes to have fun. However, some competition is healthy. Competition allows us to accomplish great things. Have you ever noticed that you generally perform at higher level with competition than you would without? The key is to have balance. To allow the competitiveness to be a positive force without crossing the line into foul play.

My Story

I've been a people pleaser and wanted to make EVERYONE happy. And guess what I learned? It is not possible no matter how hard you try. You will NEVER succeed at making everyone happy. It's more critical that you work on making YOURSELF happy first. After all, you can't give what you don't have. While I was running around trying to make everyone else happy, I personally was running on empty. But I'd be damned if I was going to give up "me" in order to assure everyone else's happiness.

Chapter 9:

Barbie's Dream House is Over-rated

Sometimes a dream is best left as that; a dream. All too often our dreams are made up of how we think others want our life to be. What mom wouldn't want to see her daughter living in the Barbie dream house with a white picket fence and 2.5 kids (I never really understood that saying)? But you know what? As much as mom may love you and as much as your friends and family want what's best for you, ultimately it is your life. The beauty of that is that you get to create and design the life that you want.

During Drama Free Divorce Detox I often ask people, "Where do you want to be in your life?" and the responses that I hear most often are:

"I just don't want to be unhappy anymore."

"I just want my old self back."

While those are perfectly good answers, both answers are what I call "no brainers" because we all want to stop hurting and we all want to be allowed to be ourselves. Both are normal responses for how you are feeling at this point in your life. When people are at a low point they will look to the next one or two levels of betterment as their goal. And that is okay. But why stop there? Now is the time to shoot for the stars. Yes, you are in a bad marriage, going through divorce or newly divorced. Yes, you can and will stop being unhappy. Yes, you can and will get back to your old self. Whew, what a relief to know that, right? There is even better news! There are no limitations to the life you create for yourself and your family. When you focus on staying true to yourself, you will automatically start to nurture the aspirations that you have always had.

My Story

During my detox I would ask myself every day, "Am I staying true to myself?" I knew that recreating my new life would not be easy. I knew that "settling" for the familiar would be much easier so it was important that I not allow that to happen. By asking myself everyday if I was doing what I needed to do in order to be true to myself, I was holding myself accountable for my forward progress. Another thing I would say daily (and I still say it) is, "May I be elegant and graceful." It didn't always work—sometimes I was a whiny bitch—but I tried my best. It's never about being perfect; it's about doing the best I could do week by week, day by day, hour by hour.

Make Me Smile

- ½ medium apple

- 1 c broccoli florets

- 2 carrots

- 1 c kale or spinach

- 1 celery stalk

Before juicing, wash all fruits and veggies. Serve juice over ice.

This recipe is chock full of vitamins A, B, C, E, beta-carotene, iron, folic acid and magnesium.

Chapter 10:

The Hamster Wheel of Life

Under the best circumstance, life is a juggling act. This is especially true as we try to balance all the obligations that we have to our children, spouse, work, keeping physically fit as well as spiritually healthy. Wrap all of that up in a heaping helping of keeping our finances on track and it is no wonder we are so damn tired.

If you are truthful with yourself you will admit that some areas are suffering because the focus is all on a select few. In order to meet our obligations at work we often sacrifice our time at the gym. In order to get everything done at home we often will sacrifice our spiritual health. In order to move forward with a life that is well balanced we need to take a look at where we feel we are at this current moment in time. This is not a look at where we want to be but it is your starting point; your baseline.

This wheel is a great visual to help you see where you are out of balance. Your goal is to be balanced at 100% in all areas so by determining your actual level you will be able to see where you need to shift your attention.

To Do: Let's make this fun! Go get some crayons, colored pencils or markers. Anything that is colorful. Towards the middle of the wheel is 0 and the outer edge is 100%. Take a few moments to honestly assess where you are in each category. Color in that section to the level that you feel is correct. If finances are at 50% than only color in half of the section.

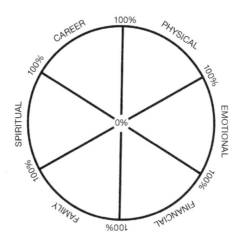

There are going to be deficiencies in different areas of your life, we all have them. However, since the purpose of a wheel is to be perfectly circular, balanced and to move forward with ease, then we have to identify the weak "spokes" in our life. Now that you have colored in your sections, imagine if this wheel were the wheel on your car. Being so out of balance it would certainly be a very uncomfortable and bumpy ride.

Keeping the goal in mind of detoxing and making the changes you need to live a life of fulfillment, I have another To-Do for you.

TO DO

This is an exercise that needs to be done when you have little or no distractions. Maybe take your morning coffee in the backyard and sit quietly or relax in your favorite chair with some nice music on in the background. I want to you read each of the sentences and reflect on them as you allow your answers to come to you. I encourage you close your eyes, take deep breaths and relax. Do not try to assess all the circumstances that surround the questions. Just give yourself permission to "feel" the answers. There is no need to write anything down. If you want to write your responses, do it after your time of reflection.

1. Where are you **emotionally?** What are the most common emotions you "live" in each day? Are they serving you? If they are not serving you in a positive way than what voids are they filling that keeps you in this emotional state?

2. Where are you **physically?** If you were to describe your current physical identity, what would it be? If you would describe your ideal physical identity, what would it be? Keeping in mind that your physical identity is not limited to your weight or to how tone your body is (although it does include those areas). It also refers to your physical health overall.

3. Where are you **financially?** Are you living day to day, paycheck to paycheck? Do you feel like you are in a huge financial hole that you can't get out of? Are you financially comfortable but would like to be more proactive in preparing for retirement? Are you financially sound in all areas both present and future?

---

4. Where is your **career?** Do you love your job and find happiness in it each day? Are you stuck in a job and have no idea how to get out of it and move forward? Is your career taking off? Do you feel as if you are not fulfilling your life's passion?

5. How about **spiritually?** Do you have a relationship with a higher being? Have you let that relationship fade due to the stress in your life? Do you feel centered and grounded? Do you most often feel anxious, disconnected, and scattered?

6. How is your **family life?** Do you consider your family and your home to be your safe haven? Are you feeling stressed about your lack of intimacy? Are you experiencing daily conflicts with your kids? Are you constantly battling with your parents or siblings? Do you have a loving, supportive, tension-free family situation?

It is very hard to take a deep inner look when you already know that you will identify shortcomings. While you may find yourself feeling bad about what you uncover, do not let it drag you down. Identifying your areas of opportunity is a great thing. It separates you from people who choose to bury their head in the sand and never take that first step towards positive change.

Chapter11:

Purging the Crap in Your Life

Now is the time to visit the process of purging things from your life that are toxic. Sometimes those "things" are actual things, sometimes they are mindsets and unfortunately, sometimes they are people. If you are committed to reclaiming your true self then you need to surround yourself with supportive people who believe in your journey and your dreams. If there are people in your life who weigh you down instead of pulling you up, you have to get rid of them. Don't panic! It is not as horrid as it seems. At this point in time people will fall into three categories:

- Keepers

- Temporary Break

- Permanent Disconnect

Keepers: The people in your life who are good for you. They are supportive, show positivity, you feel better when you are around them and you would be miserable if you didn't have them in your life.

Temporary Break: The people in your life who you just don't need to be involved with right now. It may be a dear friend who you really enjoy being with however she tends to put down your ex every time you are together. This is derailing your main goal of coming out of detox in a good place with your ex. Maybe it's a wonderful cousin who is very emotional and often ends up crying about your situation when you try to share with her. You do not want to remove these people from your life permanently however you need a vacation from them. While they are trying to be supportive they are not with the plan. Best to reconnect with them when you are happy and healthy and living your new life.

Permanent Disconnect: While you may really like this group of people you know in your heart that they were not good for you in the past, are not good for you now and will not be good for you in the future. Sometimes you need to cut your losses in order to save yourself.

Determining this is often hard to do. If I asked you to make a chart with these three categories and place people names in a column you would find that to be very challenging. No one wants to intentionally place someone in a list that can ultimately mean the end of your relationship with them. So instead of approaching it from that way we are going to approach if from a very positive way.

 You are going to love this exercise. It is eye opening and empowering. You are going to create your happiness wall. This can be some place out in the open like your refrigerator door or some place more private like your closet wall. The concept is simple. Place a photo or some image on your happiness wall anytime someone or something:

- Makes you smile

- Makes you less stressed

- Makes you feel supported

- Makes you forget your troubles for a period of time

- Encourages you

- Motivates you

- Loves you unconditionally

If your mom calls you just to check on you and it warmed your heart, add her photo to your wall. You neighbor asks you over for a glass of wine; add her to your wall. A coworker stops by your office to see if you need anything, offering a genuine smile when she asks, add her to your wall. In a few weeks you will have a clear visual of whom your keepers are and who didn't make the cut. Those who you thought about putting on their a few times but just didn't get the same type level of "happiness" quotient from them are most likely people you need a temporary break from. Anyone who never crossed your mind, pissed you off or in any other way caused negativity in your life, you really need to consider disconnecting from permanently.

TIP: If you do not have photos of people who you want to put on your wall....ask them if you can take one! Tell them how you are going to use it. They will be so honored to know that they are instrumental in your detox and healing that they will become even a bigger cheerleader than they were before.

Telling people of my decision was extremely hard. You want to believe that everyone will be on your "side" so to speak but that is not usually the case.

Thankfully my mother and my brother both stood by me. They were great support system from the very start. However, I did have many friends tell me that I was making the biggest mistake of your life. Sitting down with your friends to tell them of your decision and being met with essentially a response of "Are you a damn idiot?" can certainly take the wind out of your sails. That is why it is very important to own your decision.

Kidney Classic

- 1 – small cucumber

- 1 – stalk of celery

- ¼ - lemon (peeled)

- ½ inch – fresh ginger

- 1 handful - parsley

Wash and juice all ingredients. This juice is great for the kidneys so you may want to have two servings per day.

Chapter 12:

Purging Crap Continues – I'm Pissed Off!

In the last chapter we talked about purging people from our life either temporarily or permanently. It will come as no surprise to you that you also need to begin to purge the crappy things in your life. Some days we wake up and just wonder how many damn things are going to go wrong today. How many things are going to push my button and make me want to scream? Well, no more. Just as you purged the negative people in your life…. You are now going to purge the stuff that pisses you off! There is no room in your new life for such crap.

It is time to create an action board that represents all the shit you want to be done with. Use it to capture all the negative behaviors, people, activities and situations that brought you to the unhappy and angry place that you are now. Take a week or so to really identify as much negativity in your life as possible. I'm sure that if I asked you right now you could rattle off a dozen things that piss you off about your situation and the circumstances leading up to your decision for Detox. Start with those. Grab a stack of magazines that have lots of photos and text. Get a big poster board and begin to cut out anything that represents what pisses you off. Tape or paste it on poster board. Once you run out of immediate thoughts, let it simmer with you for a few days. If something happens one day that really pisses you off that you want to be done with… put it on the board. Keep in mind that is about you. Things that piss you off that you will no longer allow. It may be something that involves your spouse or it might not. It can be anything that fits the "I'm pissed off and I'm not going to take it anymore" category. Examples could be:

- Feeling ignored

- Arguing

- Two people together, but not speaking. Is it indifference or a lack of passion?

- Waiting for the phone to ring.

- The feeling of always walking on egg shells

- Not feeling supported

- Always feeling victimized or

- Always feeling like the nagging bitch

Include as many examples as possible. Take no longer than 2 weeks (we don't want to live in the negative) then decide what you want to do with your board. It is up to you. I chose to laminate mine because it made me feel like I was entombing the things that piss me off and they would no longer be a negative force in my life. Some people chose to burn theirs as a symbol of release and others chose to tear it up into confetti and throw it to the wind. However you choose you rid yourself of what pisses you off is completely up to you. I do suggest you make a party of it though; light a candle, open a bottle of champagne and celebrate your new life by saying out loud, "I release you. I thank you but you are no longer of service to me. I am done giving you power in my life. No More! It is Done!"

Chapter 13:

Boundaries Abound

There is something that uber successful people have that the rest of us struggle with on a daily basis; the skill of setting boundaries. At the end of your detox experience you should feel better about setting boundaries with others or perhaps more accurately stated, acknowledging that it is okay to take a stand for yourself. Remind yourself that it was a different time in your life that you would allow yourself to compromise solely in order to avoid conflict. I'm sure you can recall times when you compromised even if the compromise was at a risk or at your personal expense.

When you do not set boundaries you are actually doing the exact thing that you are trying to avoid. By compromising over and over again what you are actually doing is harboring resentment. Tolerating others that show no respect for your opinion or feelings places a wedge between the two of you. Allowing others to monopolize your time and your freedom breeds contempt.

Are you the type of woman that wants to please everyone so you compromise all the time? Are you the type of man who can be firm with some people in your life and not with others? You are not alone. Education on how to set successful boundaries is something many people could benefit from.

Begin by learning to be okay with making yourself a priority. Your needs are just as important as anyone else's needs including your children.

Once you acknowledge your own needs, be non-apologetic when letting others know. I am not talking about times when someone asks you to do something fun like go to dinner. I mean if you plan on going to yoga class and someone says that they really need you to help them do something at the same time. You made a commitment to yourself (discussed in early chapters) to take care of your health and stress so you signed up for yoga.

This is a priority. Trust me, if you say "no" they are sure to find someone else. There is no need for you to justify your answer.

Keep in mind that you trained the people around you to expect you to be at their beck and call. You may shock them; even offend them, when you take your new stance. But know this; you are not responsible for how they respond. You have a right to do and say what you want just as they have a right to like it or not. My guess is that they will not be happy about it to begin with but they will come around. Just as you trained them....so you will retrain them but this time with boundaries.

Like anything else in detox, setting boundaries is an ongoing process. You can't expect to change all your habits overnight. Is there someone that you have always admired because they have a way of saying "no" to others with courtesy? Someone you know who has boundaries that you respectfully accept? Ask that person out for coffee and pick their brain. Admit that you often feel taken advantage of and want to learn how to set and keep healthy boundaries.

Once you get past the feelings of guilt and shame, you will not allow anyone to have that effect over you ever again! Ever! Not family, not friends, and certainly not your new boyfriend or girlfriend. The truth is people respect boundaries. When you set boundaries in your relationship, there's no gray area or no room for miscommunication.

Lemonade with a Kick

- 1 – alfalfa sprouts (decent handful)

- 2" – cucumber (you won't find a 2" cuke so you will have to use half of a full size cuke)

- 1 – lemon (peeled)

- - apple (granny smith)

- 1 - piece of ginger (it's spicy so make it a small piece)

Wash all ingredients and juice. Pour over ice. Really refreshing and full of goodness such as iron, magnesium, zinc and vitamins C and K.

Part Three

Let's Get Physical

DO NOT skip this section. I know that you don't want to hear one more thing about your health. Most likely people are already commenting on the fact that you look tired, too skinny, are putting on weight or look pale. They have offered a ton of suggestions from exercise, diet and home remedies. I get it – I really do. I am asking you, pleading with you to just read this section; if only just to humor me. I promise you that you will find at least one thing in it that you will find eye opening, refreshing, informative or at the very least, supportive.

Chapter 14:

Victims of Addiction

In the first chapter we looked at the steps of grieving. If you glassed over them I encourage you to go back and really take a look at them. Right now I want to focus on one step in particular and that is #2-Pain & Guilt. This is the stage where we begin to wonder what we could have done differently. We face remorse of things we said (or didn't say) and things we did (or didn't do). Many people have a hard time tolerating this stage of grief however it is very important that you do not move on until you have fully experienced the pain and not just put a Band-Aid on it.

During this stage there was a word of caution that stated: "This is also the stage where you may seek an escape through drugs or alcohol." While we all think we are strong enough to not fall to the temptations of such addictions I will tell you that no one is exempt.

I promise that I am not preaching or judging (you will see that I was not immune when you read "my story"). I feel that I would be irresponsible if I did not discuss this because is it an uncomfortable topic that many people sweep under the carpet. I do not have a carpet-sweeper personality by any stretch of the imagination. So here we go…

There is no denying that there is something therapeutic about a glass of wine or a cocktail after a long day. During detox you may be prompted by friends and family to have a drink or two before bed to help you sleep. You may be given a few of their Rx medications to help "calm your nerves." It is a fact that many people can use alcohol, prescription drugs or even recreational drugs without addiction. The problem lies in the fact that by participating in this "Band-Aid" activity you are trying to stop feeling bad and start feeling good. When you come out of Drama Free Divorce Detox that last thing you want is to need detox treatment for a drug or alcohol problem. If in your mind you just said to yourself, "This doesn't apply to me, I only have <insert number> of drinks a week or only take <name drug> when I need to relax" than listen carefully. The frequency in which drugs and alcohol are consumed and the amount of drugs and/or alcohol consumed do not automatically give a label of addiction or abuse.

There is no magic number that indicates when drug and/or alcohol use has moved from casual to problematic. Like everything else in Drama Free Divorce Detox, it is very personalized. While one person having three drinks every other day may not be a problem at all; for someone else it can be the start down a very slippery slope. That is why I want to provide some information for you to consider.

Slow and steady often goes unnoticed. What I mean by that is that we can often slowly begin to increase the amount or frequency of use yet never give it a second thought. That glass of wine every other night can creep up to one…two …three glasses every night. That one Rx pill your friend gave you for sleep worked so well so what is the harm is taking one every night? Smoking a joint on the weekend can quickly turn to smoking 5 times a day every day. It happens so gradually we often do not even notice the problem.

Certainly a divorce leaves you feeling like your life is full of voids, black holes if you will. To avoid that "creeping" of increased alcohol or drug use it is best to try to avoid them all together. Fill the void with things of pleasure or healthy alternatives. Instead of pouring that next glass of wine, go in the backyard and throw the ball to the dog. Enjoy the smells and sounds of the outdoors.

Do what brings you happiness, escape into your painting, knitting or a good book. These are the types of "addictions" that can stay with you for a lifetime. The other negative addictions will haunt you for a lifetime.

Often, our increased use becomes a concern to others way before it becomes a concern for us. We have convinced ourselves that we can handle it, can stop at any time and that it is not affecting anyone else. We have other excuses that we use when we are late for meetings, miss appointments, when our job performance is suffering or when we are unable to socialize or meet our family obligations.

TO DO Right here, right now, I want you to make a promise to yourself! Say it silently or write it down but do it! And that promise to yourself is:

I promise that if at any point in time I feel unable to deal with my emotions, my stress, my alcohol use, my drug use or my situation in anyway, that I will seek help.

This help can be in the form of professional help, the help of clergy or other religious leaders who you trust or reaching out to a friend who you feel is a stable support. The friend should be someone who doesn't always tell you what you want to hear. When you are at the end of your rope you need people who love you enough to tell you the truth. Thank goodness I had such courageous and direct people in my life or you may not be reading this book right now.

My Story

Adapting to my new role as a newly single mom with three kids and all that it entailed emotionally, physically and financially, was tough. Throw in the fact that I also had ruptured two discs in my back and was facing a potential surgery; a very expensive one at that. Not only was I emotionally drowning but was in so much pain. I had to get relief and that relief came in the form of Panadeine with codeine.

I did not have a problem. I needed it for health reasons (or so I told myself). Until one day a dear friend had the courage to point out what I couldn't see in my initial post-divorce fog.

I was speaking in Sacramento. I was up on stage doing what I normally do and he was greatly disturbed by what he saw.

After my presentation he bluntly asked, "What is wrong with you? You're so skinny, like, in a whole other world. "

WHAT??? How the hell did he know? I thought I was fooling everybody.

I had truly reached a lifetime low. I was a mess. I was in a trance on a daily basis. Work was suffering as I turned down coaching jobs left and right. The work was there but I chose to turn my focus to more harmful things. A spiral ensues as the more work I turned down the more income I lost.

I had all the tools that I needed and all the emotional support but I still couldn't get my act together.

I am forever indebted to my friend for not sweeping what he saw under the rug. It took love and courage for him to call me out like that and thank God he did. That day changed my life!

Chapter 15:

Can The Divorce Detox Help Mend Your Broken Heart?

A divorce can have a serious impact on your health; it can actually make you physically sick. Why am I telling you this again? Because of Takotsubo cardiomyopathy. Takotsubo cardiomyopathy is the official term for a broken heart. Yep, it's true. A broken heart is a real thing. Are you as surprised as I was to find this out? Takotsubo cardiomyopathy is a heart condition that has symptoms very similar to the symptoms of a heart attack. You can find more information about it on the website of the American Heart Association, but basically a broken heart is provoked by the raised levels of adrenaline that is in our bodies when we are under excessive stress. This causes the heart to temporarily expand. It is reported that stress is the cause in nine out of ten cases of broken heart syndrome. Who knew?

More proof that the physical and emotional mind-body connection is so strong that when you are emotionally detoxing from someone, it helps to fortify your body with a physical detox or cleanse as well. While it may be easier to run to the dollar menu than to choose a healthy alternative, your body doesn't appreciate it. You need to give your body what it needs to stay healthy by taking vitamins and eating a more balanced diet. Make sure you have healthy options available for those times when your emotions start flooding in unexpectedly. Replace that gallon of ice cream with yogurt and fruit. Replace brooding with a nice walk. I will go into this in more detail in the upcoming chapters and will even share with you some of my favorite detox juices and other recipes.

Chapter 16:

No One Likes a Cootie: Keeping Stress and Illness at Bay

One piece of advice that you are probably sick of hearing is that you have to take care of yourself if you are going to remain strong. As annoying as it is to hear it repeatedly, it is true. Unfortunately, our health takes a back seat during stressful times. To say that divorce increases stress is a total understatement.

Did you know that stress is actually linked to the five leading causes of death in the United States? Cancer, heart disease, accidents, lung disease and suicides are all exacerbated by the stress in our lives. Research data shows:

- Over 75 percent of all physician visits are with patients who complain of symptoms or conditions that were associated with stress.

- Over 50 percent of people asked reported that their level of stress is affecting their health.

- Over 100 million Americans take a physician prescribed medication for stress-related symptoms.

- Stress can affect every body part or bodily system, nothing in our body is exempt.

Physically, the muscles in our body begin to feel the pressures of stress before any other body part. When we have tension in our lives our muscles will constrict causing them to become tense. A tense muscle affects nerve endings, blood vessels, organs, bones and skin. This domino affect continues with cramps, clenched jaw, chest and back pain, muscle spasms, teeth grinding and tremors.

Chronic (prolonged) stress is responsible for a physical inflammatory response in our blood vessels. Heart disease is linked to inflammation. Do you see how this cycle is playing out?

Let's not forget our immune system. It is critical that we maintain a healthy immune system in order to keep our body in homeostasis; the physical action that is responsible for assuring that our body sustains equilibrium. It is the homeostatic mechanisms that are responsible for regulating things such as body temperature, blood pressure, heart beat, our breathing and the production of blood cells. Stress is known to weaken the immune system therefore putting the homeostasis balance in jeopardy. A healthy immune system helps the body resist infection, illness and disease. When we do come down with a "cootie" our immune system jumps into action, combats the offending bug and allows us the pleasure of a speedier recovery than people with an unhealthy immune system.

Like the small snowball that rolls down the hill and becomes a gigantic boulder, uncontrolled stress rolls through our body in much the same way. While the ultimate goal is to not allow the stress to creep up on us in the first place, if (or when) it does we have to nip it in the bud and not allow it to wreak havoc.

Is that possible? Yep!

Arming yourself with healthy meals, regular exercise, a confident mindset and positive thinking gives us an advantage when it comes to warding off those "cooties." You need to remember that by exercising your mind and encouraging your mind-body connection you can be proactive in strengthening your immune system.

After my divorce I lost about fifteen pounds. My body was reacting to the stress I was putting it through. Sometimes I was a good influence on my body and other times I was not. While my diet mainly consisted of drive-thru fare I did try to make good choices by selecting things such as the green tea lemonade and a protein plate from Starbucks.

Chapter 17:

Your body is talking. Are you listening?

We discussed the effects that stress can have on our bodies. One practice to consider is the practice of traditional Chinese Medicine. Chinese Medicine is based on emotions other than stress and how they affect the body. The concept is that there are five major organ systems. These systems are paired to specific emotions.

Author Louise Hay, in her book, You Can Heal Your Body, goes into great detail about this philosophy. Hay states that our body can act as a messenger for our emotions. For example:

- The fear caused by lack of finances can result in low back pain.

- Circulation problems signifies the inability to express (and even feel) positive emotions.

- High blood pressure can be triggered by unresolved emotional problems.

- Knee problems denote mental/emotional inflexibility.

A positive approach, should you experience such symptoms, is to communicate with your body.

When you notice physical symptoms take a moment and ask, "What emotion am I feeling?"

Take note of exactly what physical response you are experiencing such as a stomach ache, headache, back, and neck or chest pain.

Educate yourself on the emotion/organ pairing and what it indicates.

Determine what action you can take to eliminate that negative emotion and begin the healing process. Generate a list of activities that make you happy and try to do them on a regular basis e.g. gardening, baking, long walks or writing.

Rekindle relationships with people who you enjoying spending time with.

Check out these examples:

Anger: Feeling Angry? Your liver and gall bladder are affected, both of which produce and store bile. Other associated emotions could be frustration, resentment and irritability. You may feel headaches, dizziness, drained in terms of energy level, and high blood pressure. Anger may also cause you to behave in ways that do not serve you, or you may choose to repress it, which is also harmful.

So what can you do? For starters, breathe. While taking deeps breaths start to shift your focus so that you begin to calm your body and resist the anger.

- What is the source of the anger? How can you reduce/ eliminate it?

- Is there a song you can play that always puts you in a good mood?

- Enjoy a cup of chamomile or other herbal, calming tea.

- Do something physical to divert the anger. Walking, jogging or any other physical activity will get those endorphins going and will allow the anger to wane.

- Go to a "happy" lunch with friends. No grumbling allowed. Talk about the awesome people, places or moments that remind you that life is a precious treasure.

Anxiety: Excessive worry can prevent a person from using energy which can impact the lungs and large intestine. You may experience a shortness of breath or digestive challenges leading to ulcerative colitis. Here's the deal. When we talk about anxiety or worry what we are really talking about is what you perceive to be reality. Worrying often leads to our imaginations running wild. What we imagine may be true or may not be true. The fact that we are focused on it makes it our reality at the time. It can be something terrible like having to have a medical test done and the whole time allowing anxiety and worry to convince you that the diagnosis will be life threatening. It can be something as simple as meeting a friend for lunch and they are late. A logical reason for their tardiness may be traffic however the longer you wait the more you assume it is a passive-aggressive move to retaliate for a misunderstanding that you thought you resolved months ago.

Shift your focus! It is important to not give into the negative reactions that are often irrational. By taking a more positive approach to such situations you are reducing the physical harm that your emotions are causing your body. You are also staying in control of the situations.

I know I sound like a broken record but another great way to shift your focus is to get physical! Go to a yoga class so that you are naturally present, feel at peace and can experience the relaxation of a meditative state. The worry and anxiety will quickly go away. You will begin to realize that you worked yourself up into a state that not only did not serve you, but may or may not have been reality. Deep breathing will help eliminate toxicity and your digestion will revert to a more regular and healthy state.

Sunny Days

- 2 – medium apples

- 2 – beet roots (apx 2" diameter)

- 1 - carrot

- 1 - orange (peeled)

- 1 – sweet red pepper

- 1 – sweet potato (apx 4-5")

Wash and juice all ingredients. Serve over ice. This recipe promotes healthy lungs and it rich in magnesium, potassium, vitamins A, B, C and K.

Part Four

Rediscovering,
Reclaiming
& Reinventing
YOU!

"Within each of us is a hidden store of energy. Energy we can release to compete in the marathon of life. Within each of us is a hidden store of courage, courage to give us the strength to face any challenge. Within each of us is a hidden store of determination. Determination to keep us in the race when all seems lost."

— Roger Dawson

Chapter 18:

Who You Are at Your Core

Whether it is rediscovering, reclaiming or reinventing, the time is now to remember who you are at your core. Your know, your core; the part that is unique but which you have sacrificed, twisted, manipulated and no longer recognize because you tried to be who others thought you should be.

 Do you remember a time in your life when you felt confident, unstoppable, maybe a little sassy and full of yourself? It doesn't have to be a particular event (although it could be); it should be a time in your life when you were on top of the world. College year's maybe? Right after you made a big decision? Find some uninterrupted time, grab a glass of wine or a hot tea and find a quiet relaxing place to sit. Take some time to relive that point in your life. Really try to remember:

- Who was in your life at that time?

- Where were you geographically?

- How would you describe yourself during that time?

- How did you feel?

- What emotions did you "live in" ….constantly experience…when you felt like nothing was going to stand in your way?

As you recall this story I anticipate that you will feel some positive waves of happiness, confidence and empowerment. Fast forward to today and ask yourself the same questions. Are you getting the answers that you want? What has changed?

Envision the "empowered you" of your past meeting the "you" now. Because of the journey that you are on, because of this place where it has brought you, you are now able to fully

---

embrace and reinvent that empowered you of days gone by. You are older, wiser and ready! You see, all along it was not only about winning the game…it was about the person that you became along the way.

So this is your time. Damn, doesn't that feel great?!?

This is the most exciting part of detox in my opinion. It is time to grab another cup of tea, a smoothie or glass of chilled coconut water. Put on some soothing music that will put you in the perfect state of self-discovery. Get out that journal and a pen because it is time to start writing! Do not over analyze - go with your heart. It is time to rediscover who you are at your core; at the very base of your being.

1. **Who are you?** What words best describe your identity. Have fun and imagine if someone dressed up as you for Halloween what type of person would they be? Are you a Soulful Sista' to your friends? Are you a Vital Vixen? Are you a Playful Princess?

2. **Who are you really?** Who is at your core? Acknowledge the brilliance of you! Are you passionate? Intense? Successful? Sensitive? Curious?

3. **What is your Mission?** We all have a mission in life. What is yours? What do you need to do to stay focused on your mission? What will it take to really own it? Who is in your life that will support your mission? Who will help you achieve your mission? Who can you bring into your life to keep you accountable?

4. **Who are you physically?** Where are you physically? How would you like to improve your physical health? Are there things about yourself that you want to change? If you did change, how do you think would you feel about yourself?

5. **What else?** What else do you want to capture about yourself? What do you love about yourself? What makes you unique and a cut above the rest? What compliment do you hear most often?

There it is! You just had a conscience awareness of who you are at your core. This can only mean one thing... time to celebrate! Take a few moments to listen to the music, take some deep breaths and embrace the reinvented YOU.

Chapter 19

You are Never Too Old For Dr. Seuss

If you have young children or young nieces and nephews, you have probably noticed that many of the children's movies often have adult humor. It is a great marketing campaign. Parents don't mind taking kids to movies if they can be entertained as well. For the cost of ticket prices these days it is absolutely necessary for movies to appeal to a wide audience. Pixar is a great example of movies that appeal to children with bright colors and silly characters as well as appealing to adults with one liners that go sailing right over the little ones heads.

The same can be said for Dr. Seuss books. Children love the insanely colorful books with odd-looking characters who live in outlandish places. Each book has an amazing life lesson which is often too advanced to be picked up by young children but if the adult is paying attention, the message will be clear.

My daughter, Asher loved the book "Oh, the Places You'll Go" and we read it over and over again. It is the story of a character in the book making a decision to leave town and ultimately encounters what is simply called, "The Waiting Place." It is the place where everyone is always waiting for something to happen. A place where time doesn't pass... similar to what it is like when we busy ourselves just to occupy our minds.

Dr. Seuss reminds us, "that you have brains in your head, feet in your shoes, and that you can steer yourself in any direction you choose." We are also told, "And when you're alone, there's a very good chance you'll meet things that will scare you out of your pants. There are some, down the road between hither and yon, that can scare you so much you won't want to go."

Perhaps the most famous line of the book, "Will you succeed? Yes, you will indeed. (98 ¾ guaranteed)." What a great reminder that in these moments, when you are scared to death and have no idea what the future holds, you have to simply commit! You have to resolve to move forward with your decision. But never fear, according to Doctor Seuss:

"So...Be your name Buxbaum or Bixby or Bray

or Mordecai Ali Van Allen O'Shea,

you're off to Great Places!

Today is your day!

Your mountain is waiting.

So... get on your way!"

Seuss doesn't tell us exactly what our mountain will look like or how we go about getting it moved. But he does assure us that we're headed to a great place and that our journey awaits us. That's all the certainty we will get, and it's up to us to have faith and embrace it.

After reading this story to my daughter, what seemed like a million times, I realized something. I wasn't reading it for her. I was reading it for me. Sometimes the Waiting Place is the scariest place. What is your waiting place? Are you still waiting for the phone to ring? Waiting for something to change? Waiting for someone to make your decision for you?

"Oh the Places You'll Go" may technically be a classified as a children's book but it is one of the number one gifts that people give to high school and college graduates. If you do not own a copy I highly recommend you head to your local book store, grab to a nice cup of coffee and treat yourself to a copy of it as a Detox gift. Read it often. Embrace the message.

Never Grow Up

- 6 - cabbage leaves

- 6 - medium carrots

- ½ -1" - piece of ginger root

Wash all ingredients and juice. Serve over ice. This juice has anti-aging properties and is full of beta-carotene, iron, magnesium, selenium, zinc and vitamins A, B, and C.

Chapter 20:

Time for Your Fire Walk!

Everything which led up to this moment has been very important. It was critical to face reality, make the hard decisions, go through the grieving, have those tough conversations and make a vow to yourself that from this point on you deserve to be and will be happy. You will no longer remain stuck while the toxins continue to build inside of you.

So it's time to take the first step. Like doing a Fire-walk, you gotta step onto the coals and take that first step to transforming your life. It is the only way that you will ever know what it feels like to be free and live a life of fulfillment.

Inspiration can be found in many places. We often find inspiration in the lyrics of songs, in books, in people within our community and even in "famous" people. I want you to think about who you would consider to be an inspiration when it comes to life changes. Look for:

- A role model who has been through a "detox" and made it happen.

- Someone who doubted at first yet was successful. Maybe it is a person who doubted they could ever lose weight but with will and determination they succeeded.

Here are a couple of "inspiration" stories I would like to share with you. I'm pretty sure you have heard of both of them however you may not be familiar with their story of awesomeness.

J.K. Rowling: Role Model of Determination

A great role model of determination is J.K. Rowling, the creator and author of the Harry Potter series. It was in 1990 that Rowling first conceived Harry; the boy who discovered he was a wizard. It took a full seven years for that boy to fully come to life in the form of her first book in the series.

After the death of her mother, Rowling headed to Portugal where she married and became a teacher. Less than a year later she found herself not only divorced but also unemployed. Rowling shares how she struggled to provide food her herself and her daughter and resorted to living in a mice-infested apartment. Her only income was a welfare check of £70 ($111) a week. She couldn't afford to heat her flat so she regularly stayed warm by hanging out in cafes. It was there that she continually visited the idea of the boy wizard, Harry Potter. According to Rowling, "I was as poor as it is possible to be in modern Britain without being homeless. But rock bottom became a solid foundation on which I rebuilt my life.

Although an amazing success now, did you know that Harry Potter and the Philosopher's Stone was actually rejected over ten times? Today, the Harry Potter series is the best-selling book series in history. Hers is a *rags to riches* story during which she went from living on state benefits to becoming a multi-millionaire in five years' time. Rowling is currently ranked the twelfth wealthiest woman in the United Kingdom.

Mark Burnett: Letting Go of the Shit Leads to Legendary Success

Another great example of letting go of the s#&t is television producer **Mark Burnett**. At age seventeen, he enlisted in the British Army from 1978-1982, and became a Section Commander in the Parachute Regiment. In October 1982, at the age of 22, Burnett decided to immigrate to the U.S. where he met up with a friend, Nick Hill, who had emigrated from Britain a few years earlier and was working as a nanny and chauffeur. Hill knew of an open position for a live-in nanny with the Jaeger family in Beverly Hills. Although he had no experience in that field, Burnett took the opportunity. Because of his military background, the Jaegers took advantage of the opportunity to have a two-in-one nanny and security for their children. He eventually moved on to another family in Malibu. His responsibilities started out as the caregiver to two children for $250 and turned into a position in the father's insurance agency. Burnett took as second job selling tee-shirts in Venice Beach on the weekends.

In 1991, Burnett participated in Raid Gauloises; an adventure competition. It was then that Burnett saw a business opportunity. He purchased the rights and that is how **Eco-Challenge** made its way to America. You could say that Eco-Challenge launched Burnett's career in television production.

Burnett is now the executive producer of five network television series which air in over 70 countries. *The Bible, Celebrity Apprentice*, Shark Tank, Survivor and The Voice are all credits on Burnett's impressive. I bet her never would have imagined being named one of the world's most influential people by TIME Magazine, winning four **Emmy Awards** and winning four People's Choice Awards. I think it is safe to say that Burnett pushed through and seized the opportunity to move forward into greatness.

You are probably thinking that these are extreme examples and maybe they are…. Or maybe they aren't! The point is that they had roadblocks at every turn. They had self-doubt at times. They had people thinking that the path they were on was not "responsible." Like all of us, they had baggage. So if you've been hanging on to the S#&T longer than you should have, then it's time to get rid of it. It is time to calm your fears or disempower your limiting beliefs. Start your fire-walk now by taking that all important first step.

Chapter 21:

Truth: You're Gonna Feel Worse Before You Feel Better.

In fact there is a good chance that at various points you will feel like total crap. Just when you think you identified an issue and conquered it, another one will pop up. Detox is very much like an onion, once you peel back the layers, more show up. Some will make you cry and some won't but in the end you get to enjoy the flavor.

Remember what Jamie Greene said about taking these journeys and looking at them as adventures not letting them get you depressed? This is a great time to really take that information to heart. One part of the divorce process that seems to weigh people down is the fact that it feels like it will never end; that there is no light at the end of the tunnel. But there is! Look at each experience individually and know that you are going to go through dark times and just when you think it can't get any darker. BAM! You made it through and are basking in the brightest light of empowerment ever. I am reminded of this every time I fly into Las Vegas as night. For hours it is pitch black. You think the flight is never going to end. The captain announces that he is starting the decent but still it is pitch black. Then you blink and WOW...the lights of Las Vegas light up the sky.

There will be times when you will most likely feel regret. You will be tempted to go back to the way things were. You will wonder if you should give up your search for the renewed you and go back to the complacency of being in you comfort zone.

You may not be happy there but you know what to expect; going back to what you know. You may begin to wonder, "If making this huge change is causing me pain and anxiety than why should I even bother." First of all, because the pain and anxiety that you feel during detox is one of healing. That is very different that the stagnant pain and anxiety you feel in a bad relationship. Secondly, you need to begin to grow. You want more than just to settle for being …just being. You need to continue to look for that life that is filled with happiness and opportunity.

It may make the detox process a bit easier and a bit less scary if you look at the Four Stages:

The Awakening: This is when you realize you've been "napping" when it comes to your life. You have been going through your hours, days, week, months and years just going through the motions. You have finally reached a threshold of pain and decided to commit to change.

Conditioning: This is about what not to bring into your life as you move forward. You become more perceptive about how you want to fill your schedule, what emotions you will feel and which emotions you will reject, and even simple things such as what you'll put on your refrigerator; those things you'll see daily on a regular basis. A great resource is, Organize Yourself! A book co-authored by Ronni Eisenberg and Kate Kelly. It will provide you with ideas for how to organize areas of your life. It will also teach you how to make decisions about what you want to keep in your life and what you need/want/are ready to eliminate.

The Detox: This is basically "Emptying the Pantry." Ridding yourself of relationships and anything else that has become toxic in your life. It eliminates all things and people that are weighing you down and sucking the vitality out of your life.

Replacing the Old with the New: This is where you make decisions about what you want to replace from the past and how you want to enhance your future. This could include:

- The emotions you experience.

- How you communicate with others.

- The boundaries you want to put in place.

- Your lifestyle choices.

- The friends you choose to associate with.

- The food you chose to eat.

- The exercise routine you want to follow.

- The financial dreams you're going to pursue.

For me this is the fun part. Isn't it fun knowing that you get to create a simple plan for making all this happen? This is when you stop feeling like crap and begin to embrace the excitement of writing your new destiny. It's when you decide what you'd like to achieve in the next 30-40 days. Maybe it is more natural for you to sync your plan with the four seasons. And you get to determine if your journey will be on the slow, medium or fast track. A great reference that you may want to check out is The Total Health Makeover by Marilu Henner, http://www.marilu.com/thm.php, in which she offers a 10-Step, 30 Day Plan.

To Do: Create Your Own "Care Package" – this is a fun way to remind yourself of your transformation and to support your efforts. The content as well as the package itself should be something that makes you feel happy. The package can be a basket that you admire or a box that you've decorated and it should instantly change the way you feel just by looking at it and knowing it is there. A feeling of lightness, joy and freedom! Some items you may want to include:

- A candle to light when you feel you are headed to a dark place.

- Bubble bath! Ease your mind and your body with a warm bath of your favorite fragrance.

- A framed photo of you having fun with friends.

- Some of your favorite CD's with music to soothe your mind and soul (uplifting not deflating)

- A fuzzy afghan or throw that you can cuddle under to warm your body and heart.

- A gift card from your favorite store to remind you that you deserve abundance and gifts!

Great books that you can refer to such as:

- Horton Hears a Who! by Dr. Seuss

- The Total Health Makeover by Marilu Henner

- Organize Yourself! by Ronni Eisenberg and Kate Kelly

- What About Me? by Dr. Jane Greer

- The Best Year of Your Life by Debbie Ford

- Excuse Me, Your Life is Waiting by Lynn Grabhorn

- Move Your Stuff, Change Your Life by Karen Rauch Carter

- Splits of champagne for a glass or two to celebrate the new you!

Why not share the "care" and create a few care packages for other people who you know are going through hard times. It is important for everyone to have ample information, tools, and skills to help stay the course; especially during the challenging times that may come up unexpectedly. It will also do a lot for your confidence when you begin to feel strong enough to show support for others.

Grape Cheers

- 2 c - blackberries

- 2 c – grapes (purple or black)

- 2" pc - ginger root

Wash and juice all ingredients. Serve over ice. This juice is good for digestion and as an anti-inflammatory. It is rich in manganese, potassium and vitamins B, C and K

Chapter 22:

The Power of Positive Thinking; Affirmation Style

As soon as you read the word "Affirmations" you may be tempted to skip this "hippie shit." DON'T! Give me a chance to explain because this is key to good mental health not only during detox but in life. So what is affirmation or self-talk? It is making you a priority. When we talk to others we generally are sensitive to their feelings. When we talk to ourselves we don't tread so lightly. We have no problem stomping all over our own feelings. It is equally important (if not more) to communicate with ourselves with the same positivity, motivation and respect.

Using positive affirmations is one tool that I highly recommend. These short statements can be spoken, written or thought to create your reality. When we intentionally have healthy thoughts we can begin to influence our subconscious mind. This will serve to boost your immune system and improve your overall health and body performance.

Affirmations may include present, future of general statements. Samples of affirmations that can be used for health and wellness:

- My attitude is the most positive it has ever been
- I will resist stress
- My mind and body are in harmony
- I am a powerhouse
- I will work to build a strong foundation

- My body is becoming healthier every day
- I am beginning to feel more empowered
- I can recover quickly

Listen to this interesting tidbit. A research study came out of Carnegie Mellon University in Pennsylvania. During the study 193 adults recorded their positive/negative emotions. After a two week timeframe, all the participants were exposed to the flu virus or the common cold. The research data reports that fewer cold, flu and respiratory symptoms were reported by those participants with optimistic outlooks versus the higher illness rate of the more negative participants.

The mind-body connection is an amazing thing. It is also one thing that we tend to forgo in times of stress. There is no better time than now to put your belief system into practice. Often when we struggle we often turn our backs on the one thing that we should be bringing closer; whether that is the power of prayer, mediation and communicating with the universe. The excuse I hear most often is that there is just not enough time. I hear ya… there are never enough hours in the day. That is why we have to find time or create time. I know you just chuckled or rolled your eyes but hear me out. First, let me tell you something that I heard and it has stuck with me for many years.

A parishioner went up to her priest and asked, "Father, is it ok if I fold laundry while I pray?" and the priest responded, "When praying it is best to devote all your attention to God." She then asked another priest the same question but in a different way, "Father, is it ok if I pray while I'm folding laundry?" to which he replied, "Of course! God loves any moment that we can find time to communicate with him."

When we look at it like that we DO have time. We can find time. While I don't suggest you go into deep meditation on your long drive to work. I do think that is a great time to mentally say your daily affirmations. It is all about pushing out the negative mindset that seems to materialize when we are doing mundane tasks and replacing it with positive and healthy thoughts.

This section is so important is it worthy of two.

Think about your day to day routine and pick three times of the day where you can incorporate positive thinking/prayer/mediation/affirmations. As we saw in the story of the "praying during laundry" story, it does not need to be quiet dedicated time.

Create three affirmations that you want to focus on to start. To help you do this, explore where you are struggling the most or what you are worried about the most. Example: If you are struggling more with remaining positive in front of the children and are not eating properly. You may want to use "I am strong and will support my children with my strength" and "My body is my foundation. I will provide it with the tools to keep me healthy".

Bunch of Berries

- 1 c - blackberries
- 1 c - blueberries
- 1 c - raspberries
- 1 c - strawberries

Wash all fruit and juice. Serve over ice. Great for mental clarity and digestion, this juice is high in antioxidants, folic acid, iron and vitamins A, B, C & E

Chapter 23:

Living the Vision

Have you ever thought about making a vision board (or as some prefer to call it, an "action" board)? Too many people just think about creating their vision board, they think about what type of things they would put on it and they plan to get around to it…one day. Well guess what? There is no better time like the present.

So what exactly is a vision board? Essentially, a vision board is a custom collage made up of things that represent what you would like to achieve, to do or to have. It represents your goals and dreams. Your vision board will help train your subconscious mind, letting it know what your goals are and how you would like to accomplish them. It also puts those goals out into the universe.

How to use a vision board? Many people think that just because it is called a "vision" board that you are supposed to look at it as a reminder of what you want in life. While there is certainly no harm in having a visual reminder, the proper use of a vision board is so much more. A vision board is about "seeing" yourself as you would be upon achieving that goal. It is about feeling, really feeling, as if you have already achieved the goal. It is about taking note of how having achieved this goal makes you feel. Are you happier? More confident? The "as if" feeling (meaning, "as if" I have already achieved my goal) is what triggers the Law of Attraction. It attracts the goal and the means by which you achieve the goal and provides the opportunity for your dreams and goals to become your reality.

How to create a vision board? The first thing you need is to take a hard look at what reality you are trying to attract. What is important to you? Which goals do you want to accomplish? Once accomplished, will reaching these goals make you feel happy and fulfilled? If you don't have an immediate idea, a great place to start would be to look back that the Hamster Wheel of Life exercise. Are there portions of your life you feel you need to set goals for in order to have positive growth? That would be a perfect place to start. Once you have determined your vision board goals, be as specific as possible. Remember, this is not how you are going to achieve it but rather what it looks like once you have achieved it. For example, all this divorce crap has left you feeling as if you have lost connection with your children. You are determined to begin to spend more quality time with them to strengthen the bond. One your board you may choose to add pictures of a family at the beach or park. A picture of a mom reading to her child. An actually photo of your family doing something they used to love to do; something you want to recapture. You can also add pictures of how achieving this goal would make you feel by adding pictures of smiles or hearts. You can help the inspiration of your board by adding affirmations or quotes that relate to your goals. Here are a few examples of vision/actions boards that I have created:

For those of you who prefer a more "techie" vision board, there is software available specifically for creating your vision board. Once it is created you can save it as your wall paper, screen saver or you can print it out so you still have a visual source around your home or office.

Sharing your goals with others will help to keep you accountable. By showing your support system your board they will have a better understanding of what you desire as your end result.

Your vision board is personal and unique. There is no right or wrong way to go about creating one. It is ever-changing. As you achieve your goals, update your board to reflect your new focus. The important thing is that you put your true self into it with positive energy. This energy will flow out into the universe and help you achieve your dreams and goals.

Chapter 24:

Transformational Language...Words to Infuse Into Your Life

The art of wording is one that every person should strive to master. All too often, we don't realize that the words we use in our lives can shift how we feel, how we show up with other people and how we choose to design our lives. The words we choose send us a message. It can be a strong message of motivation and conviction or a wishy-washy message of doubt and hesitation.

Let me give you an example. You and I are out enjoying lunch together and we are having a discussion about how important it is to make time for yourself every day. You say to me:

I am trying to get up 30 minutes early every day so I can start my day with peaceful meditation.

This is great! I would be so happy about the fact that you have decided to embrace meditation as a way to start to your day on a positive note yet I'm not convinced about your sincerity. However, if you were to say to me:

I am committed to getting up 30 minutes early every day so I can start my day with peaceful meditation.

BAM! I am sold. I know that you have embraced the importance of "me" time and have made a firm commitment to make it happen. The thing is, if I was not convinced with your "try" sentence than either were you. By using words like "try" you are actually giving yourself a very easy out should you choose not to follow through with your efforts.

Other weak words that you need to consider are should, hope and want.

"Should" is very similar to "try." You could say, "I should get up 30 minutes early so that I can start my day with peaceful meditation. You can easily replace "should" with "will" to make it a strong sentence of commitment.

"Intend" is a good replacement word for "hope." Some people feel confused about this because having hope or being hopeful is a good thing, right? Yes. However, when you use "hope" in an example such as, "I hope I get to take a vacation this year" it still lacks conviction. "I intend to take a vacation this year" shows ownership and holds more power.

Another passive word is "want." If you were to say, "I want to start holiday shopping early this year" it sounds as if it is going to be followed up with an excuse. "I want to start holiday shopping early this year….. but I say that every year and never do. Use a strong word that proclaims your decision, "I am going to start holiday shopping early this year."

Chapter 25:

You are What You Speak

In the previous chapter I showed you how your word choice can give you ownership of your statements and actions. Now I want to show you how powerful it can be to actually feel your word choices. If I ask you say the word "tree" you immediately see a tree in your mind as you say it. You can see the bark, the branches and the leaves. Say the word "grace" and I bet you didn't imagine an actual thing, instead you felt the word. By incorporating these feeling words into your vocabulary on a regular basis you are telling your mind and body that enjoy the way they make you feel. These feelings will soon become the norm in your life and not the exception.

- **Centered** – gives feelings of self-confidence, goal-oriented, and well-balanced.

- **Commit** – gives the feeling of being decisive not indecisive. It is a pledge to yourself.

- **Courage** – gives the feeling that you are capable; stable in mind and spirit to face difficulty, danger, pain etcetera in spite of your fear.

- **Decide** – gives the feeling of being settled with a plan and confident in your ability to adhere to it.

- **Elegance** – gives the feeling of being graceful in appearance, behavior and movement.

- **Faith** – gives the feeling of a strong and unshakeable belief in something.

- **Forgiveness** – gives the feeling of relief and freedom; freedom of grudges, anger and pain.

- **Fulfillment** – gives the feeling of satisfaction and accomplishment.

- **Grace** –gives the feeling of peaceful gratitude.

- **Grounded** – gives the feeling of a solid foundation.

- **Passion** – gives the feeling of strong and powerful emotion.

- **Reclaim** – gives the feeling of taking back control.

TO DO

My invitation is for you to be aware of the words that you use on a daily basis. Decide if there are others that may serve you better or bring you closer to the reinvention of YOU! This list offers a few suggestions. Please add others and begin to create your own private vault of meaningful, impactful and powerful words.

Beautiful Dreamer

- 2 – medium apples

- 2 – med/lg kale leaves

- 1 – handful of parsley

- 1 c - spinach

Juice and serve over ice. This yumminess is rich in beta carotene, calcium, vitamins A, C, K and antioxidants.

Chapter 26:

Exposing Your True Identity

A mission statement is a staple for many businesses and organizations but did you ever consider doing a mission or identity statement for your life? It makes perfect sense since a mission statement is used as a guide to spell out your goals, provides a clear path and helps to guide decision-making. It is a declaration of where you see your place in the world and what legacy you want to leave. What a fabulous way to put into writing a statement of your values, beliefs and to show the world the person you are committed to becoming.

One of the drawbacks that people see in building an identity statement is that life moves so fast. The key is to keep the statement broad enough so that you don't have to change it weekly yet detailed enough to keep you accountable. Tap into your spiritual core as a way to discover what is important to you. Listen to your inner voice for inspiration.

An identity statement is an ever changing item in your life. As you change, grow, discover new things about yourself and reach your goals, your mission statement will also evolve. It is important to revisit your identity statement from time to time. You should look to it for guidance and make sure that it still reflects who you are and where you are going in life.

Chapter 27

Putting the Fun in Feng Shui

Now that we have talked about how to renovate your mind, health, body, attitude and your approach to life, it is time to take a look at your surroundings. While your environment at home and at work may provide you with a level of comfort and security, most likely it is arranged and decorated to be visually appealing to others. If you knew that your surrounding would have an effect on your physical health, mental health, your relationships and even your success in life, would you give more consideration to your decorating style? As you read this section, I ask that you to have an open mind.

Feng Shui studies how the placement of furniture, possessions and even yourself essentially determines every level of your life experiences. It is the belief that objects can influence personal energy flow. Personal energy flow impacts how people think and act. By having an effect on thoughts and actions it stands to reason that it can also affect how well the person performs; having a direct effect on personal and professional success.

Let's talk about the positive effects that Feng Shui can have on your life.

Feng (meaning wind) Shui (meaning water) is grounding and as a result it can help you achieve your goals. We cannot dispute that both wind and water are the two "must have" elements in sustaining life. Wind (aka air) is of course necessary for breathing and without water we would die within a matter of days.

Chi is another word many people have heard of but may not be familiar with its meaning. Chi by definition is the "natural energy of the universe" or "life force". This means that both wind and water are direct carriers of chi. When you begin to incorporate Feng Shui into your life you will start to build harmony with the flow of chi throughout your environment which in turn will enrich your personal chi or life force.

I encourage you to learn more about Feng Shui. In the Your Go-To Resources section you will find a great starting point for your exploration.

Chapter 28:

You Are Positively Glowing

By now we know that divorce and the stress it brings can have a negative effect on your body. What happens as you move forward, stress is reduced and you are feeling better every day? Then what? It is as important to maintain your physical well-being as it is your mental well-being. This chapter and several after it will shed some light on health related topics that may or may not be familiar to you. I encourage you to consider all the suggestions. There is a good chance that you are already comfortable with all these practices although they may have fallen by the wayside. You may be thinking, "Ugh, this hippie dippie crap" and that is okay too. I just ask that you read it and consider it. Your mind and body will thank you.

Chapter 29:

Yoga – Namaste My Friend

You may have noticed that even though yoga is over a thousand years old its popularity has hit an all-time high. Maybe it's because all the cool kids are doing it or maybe it's because we, as a society, are becoming more enlightened as to its benefits. The benefits of yoga are indeed vast. They encompass many things including calmness, flexibility, mental clarity, relaxation, strength, stress management and overall health.

Yoga is a great component when working on the mind-body connection; helping the mind and body to work harmoniously. It also is a fabulous way to prevent illness and injury as well as assist with recovery of current illness or injury. There are so many health benefits from yoga that it is impossible to list them all but here is a partial list:

- Decrease Blood Pressure

- Increase muscle tone

- Relieve sleeplessness

- Greater flexibility

- Better breathing

- Improve energy

- Balanced metabolism

- Weight loss

- Improved cardio & circulatory health

- Heightened spiritual awareness

You may already be participating in yoga however many people shy away from it simply because they feel overwhelmed.

With a yoga studio on every corner and all the various types of yoga, how does anyone ever figure out what it right for them? I'm going to help you out. First let me lay a yoga myth to rest:

You do not have to be a super fit athlete, fitness guru or gym rat to practice yoga.

The wonderful thing about yoga is that it is completely adaptable. Most forms of yoga have modified options to the poses and movements which allows anyone to participate regardless of physical capability

I compiled this list in hopes that you will give yoga a try. A short description accompanies the yoga style however any yoga studio will be more than happy to give you additional information.

- **Anusara Yoga:** This form of yoga integrates physical alignment with positive philosophy. Perfect for any fitness level.

- **Ashtanga/Astanga Yoga:** This form of yoga is for more experienced yoga participants. It has a high physical demand associated with the continuous movement, fast pace and intensity.

- **Bikram Yoga:** A popular form of yoga with many in the Hollywood set. Also known as "hot yoga" Bikram is done in a studio room which is approximately 100 degrees. It is a complete workout which focuses on flexibility, muscle endurance and strength as well as weight loss. The intense heat is also known to be useful in detoxing the body.

- **Chair yoga:** this form of yoga allows the poses to be done with the support of a chair. An excellent choice for beginners, the elderly, the injured and anyone with restricted mobility.

- **Hatha yoga:** This form of yoga is great for beginners due to it easy-to-learn style. It is the basis for all other yoga styles. This is a perfect combination of breathing techniques, poses and meditation. Hatha yoga is a great way to achieve mental calmness and clarity.

- **Integral Yoga:** This form of yoga is very similar to Hatha yoga in that it includes breathing techniques, poses and meditation however it has the added component of prayer, chanting and a focus on self-awareness. It is also a good choice for beginners of all fitness levels. Integral is perfect if you desire a more spiritual journey through your yoga workout.

- **Iyengar Yoga:** This is also a great form of yoga for beginners, the elderly, the disabled, those with limited mobility or injuries. It incorporates blankets, cushions, towels, blocks and straps to help those with limited flexibility.

- **Jivamukti Yoga:** Not a good choice for beginners due to the physical intenseness. If you are already a yoga veteran and desire a spiritual journey as well, this may be for you. A strong emphasis on chanting, meditation, scripture vegetarianism and devotion to God makes this a great physical, mental and spiritual balance.

- **Kripalu Yoga:** Another gentle form of yoga which is often called "the yoga of consciousness" Kripalu focuses on poses held for extended lengths of time to allow emotional/spiritual blockages to be released.

- **Restorative Yoga:** A good yoga for beginners where blankets, blocks, and pillows are used to permit muscles to fully relax.

I think all of us have begun an exercise program or joined a gym only to quit weeks or months later. Most often it is not due to laziness but because the choice was not a good fit for us. It is hard to stick with anything that doesn't compliment your goals and beliefs. That is why the wide selection of yoga studios and classes are a great way to explore this health benefit.

When choosing a studio you want to be sure that you feel welcomed by the staff the minute you walk through the door. No bad vibes. As far as the yoga instructors, in my experience the vast majority are friendly and approachable. You will feel encouraged, motivated and supported. Instructors are highly trained and experienced so do not be afraid to ask any and all questions.

You do not have to commit off the bat. Most studios offer a one time trial session at discounted rates. Do it! Take advantage of the discounted (sometimes free) introductory session which will allow you to try out a variety of studios in your city. Ask if the studio offers extras such as family yoga, education sessions, health and wellness workshops or any other type of special events.

If you have been resistant to the idea of yoga, I really want to encourage you to check it out. Give it a try. The benefits are amazing and only good things can come from it.

Chapter 30:

Juicing: For the Health of It

So many things come and go, especially in the diet fad world. Who hasn't tried the soup diet, the cabbage diet, the sugar detox and so much more? Let me say right here right now that I did not add this section to discuss weight. I simply wanted to point out that through juicing you can actually use targeted recipes to help with specific health issues. If you are a fan of juicing already I think you will find the recipes to be a delicious addition to your regular routine. If you are thinking, "Oh no, Loren has gone hippie on us again" then please hear me out.

We all know that the majority of us (and most of our children) do not get nearly enough good nutrients in our daily diet. If we followed the current guidelines our dinner plates would be one-half of fruits and vegetables. Many adults can't eat that many veggies in one sitting and you can forget about even putting that many veggies in front of kids.

Between lack of time, busy schedules and stress it is hard to focus on giving our bodies the right foods that it needs in order to keep us healthy. In a world of fast food drive-thru and all-you-can-eat buffets, it is much easier to grab a quick (and cheap) meal then to cook a healthy meal or even clean/chop/ toss the ingredients for a decent salad. I know that I am preaching to the choir here. I'm sure in the past week you have grabbed a bag of chips or a soda knowing you should make a better choice but feeling you don't have the luxury of time or effort.

It is important that we discover whole food based nutrition. If we are going to have a chance a living a healthier life (not to mention a longer life) we must put an emphasis on consuming more fruits and vegetables. It is proven that proper nutrition can deliver the protection your body needs through powerful antioxidants. The National Cancer Institute states that antioxidants are "substances that may protect cells from the damage caused by unstable molecules known as free radicals. Examples of antioxidants include beta-carotene, lycopene, vitamins C and E and other substances. Many of these antioxidant substances come from fruits and vegetables."

So why aren't more people jumping on the juice bandwagon?

a) The juice looks gross

b) It is expensive

c) It is time consuming

d) People will think I'm weird

e) All of the above

Let me address these issues: Yes, people may think you are weird. Yes, often the juice looks gross (but tastes amazing), No, it is not more expensive. No, it is not any more time consuming than driving to a fast food joint, ordering and eating. So now what is your excuse? ☺

You do not have to invest a lot on juicers. I have a friend who found a great one at one of the big chain stores on sale at half price. It only cost her $49 and she uses it daily. She is amazed at how easy it is to juice, how yummy it is, how easy cleanup is and her annual physical had her physician singing her praises. I call that a good investment.

Here is an example of a juice recipe that is great for your mental clarity. The strawberries in this combination contain folic acid which is found to improve focus and concentration, help your memory and increases the ability for your brain to process information. Did I mention YUM?

Brain Juice

- 2 - large apples

- ½ - peeled lime

- 3 c -strawberries (with stems)

Wash all ingredients and juice. Serve over ice. Simple as that!

At the end of the book you will find a ton of recipes in the "Your Go-To Resources" section. It is also fun to experiment with flavors. Have a fun family night or girl's night in and let each person create-their-own juice combo. Have them name it and write their recipe on a recipe card so they can duplicate their concoction again and again.

Chapter 31:

Music to Calm the Savage Beast

Fun fact: The phrase "music can calm the savage beast" was originally written as "Music has charms to sooth a savage breast". The phrase by William Congreve, is over 300 years old, appearing in 1697 in The Mourning Bride:

"Musick has Charms to sooth a savage Breast,
To soften Rocks, or bend a knotted Oak."

Music can certainly have an influence on your emotions. Some songs are calming, others can be motivational and others can be downright depressing. There is also no doubt that music has a magical way of transporting us back to a memory. The song, "I Go Back" by Kenny Chesney is a perfect example with his lyrics of "I heard it today and I couldn't help but sing along... Cause every time I hear that song....I go back to..."

One role you may not have considered music to play in your life is that of "support system." Somehow workouts seem easier with a good selection on our iPod and long road trips seems like a hop, skip and a jump with the right tunes.

So why not let music support you during your Detox? We know it has a special power to move us and stir our emotions. Imagine finding strength to handle a debilitating moment just by listening to a certain song. It can help your focus, anxiety, stress, and can be a complete mood booster. It is also proven to physically lower heart rate, blood pressure and help relieve pain while improving the quality of life.

The next time you're feeling anxious or stressed, or even angry, listen to a song or two and experience an instant shift in the way you're feeling, both emotionally and physically. Have fun creating customized playlists for times when your emotions need a little lift. Do not choose to listen to songs of woe which will only fuel your negative emotions. Empower yourself with uplifting music and before you know it you will be in a more positive state of mind.

Music can motivate you as you:

- are getting ready for the day

- feel like crying your eyes out

- are feeling grateful

- are struggling with self-worth

- are pissed off

- feel anxious

- are over being stressed

- want to bring your sexy back

- are ready to spring into action

Any genre of music you enjoy listening to, be it classical, rock, country, gospel or Gregorian chants all have a broad range of emotional selections. You will be sure to find something that makes you feel a flutter in your stomach, a wiggle in your step and even put a smile on your face.

I would venture to say that everyone reading this book listens to music in their car but how many of you have music playing at home or in the office? This week, find a way of bringing music into your life at times that do not include going 70 mph down the highway. All cable companies offer music channels that are as easy to get to as turning on your television. Use ITunes to give your iPod a music makeover. Delete all your sorrow-filled songs. You can reload them at a later time in your life when they have less meaning and impact.

Part Five

You Are
An Ever Changing
Piece of
Awesomeness!

How many times have you heard someone say that they do not like change? Maybe you heard yourself say it. Change is often viewed as a time of turmoil or upset. People feel unsettled during times of change and that is perfectly normal. The thing to remember is that unsettled isn't always a bad thing. To use a very simple analogy.....You go to bed and get all snuggled in..... you are happy and comfortable... during the night that position is no long perfect... you do a little tossing and turning....after which you have found a new position and are once again happy and comfortable. If we look at change in that way it is not such a bad thing. By "tossing and turning" at points in our life we can begin to forge new paths, meet new people and make new discoveries that lead us to new places of happiness and comfort.

That is the journey that you are on now and will be on as long as life continues. You are an ever changing piece of awesomeness. Embrace every minute of it!

Chapter 32:

So Where the Hell are You at Now? Where were You Then?

WOW! What a difference 25 chapters has made. Can you believe the capability for transformation that has occurred from the start of the book to now? While you have not put everything into play, your mindset is very different than it was in the beginning. Don't believe me?

The introduction of the book consisted of answering five questions. I asked you to hold onto those to refer to later. Well, I'd love for you to dig them out now. Read your answers.

Now, answer them again.

Some answers may have changed and some may have stayed the same. I would venture to say that some are a lot easier to answer now than they were in the beginning. That, my friend, is called growth and you should be very proud of yourself.

I encourage you to reread parts of the book as needed. Revisit the exercises. Most of all, don't try to force things. Too often we try to gauge, "Am I happy yet?" which is counterproductive. Don't try to calculate your happiness, just enjoy the journey. Before you know it you will have a hard time remembering a time when you were unhappy.

Chapter 33:

Back on the Market; Dating Again

Yes, I'm going there. You may not want to talk about it yet but someday (maybe soon) you will want to truly move on and begin building relationships both platonic and romantic. A key component of your Detox is completely letting go of the relationships that exacerbated the toxicity. You need to begin creating a warm and loving space for new relationships to come into your life. Perhaps the final part of Reclaiming happens when you are ready to ask the question: When can I date again?

For many of you, dating can be an uncomfortable process. Others may find it scary as hell. Others may be ready to jump back into the dating pool. If you are releasing a long-time intimate relationship, it may have been quite some time since you opened yourself up and allowed yourself to be vulnerable. A simple conversation with someone to whom you may be attracted can spawn butterflies in your stomach and awaken the fear of rejection. Just remind yourself that it is a process. A considerable amount of time has lapsed, this new dating scene is unfamiliar and quite frankly you are a bit rusty.

We often wonder what is the appropriate time frame be consider dating again. Here is the concrete rule: When you are ready and not a minute before! Please take that to heart. It is not when your friends think you are ready and it is not when your mom tries to fix you up with someone. It is not when you see that your ex has joined the dating pool. I will say it again…. The time to begin dating is when you are ready and not a minute before! On the other hand, what if you are ready way before those around you think is appropriate? I repeat. The time to begin dating is when YOU are ready. In many marriages the emotional divorce happened long ago so the legal divorce is just a formality making the need for "time" is lessened.

Here are a few tips to consider:

- Sometimes it is best to just go about your life and see who shows up. What I mean by that is instead of asking friends if they know of single guys or going on a blind date that your cousin set you up on, just wait and see what happens naturally.

- When you do start dating, remember that your date is not your ex. He is not responsible for anything that you have been through in the past nor is he guilty of any transgressions towards you. He has a clean slate and should be treated as such.

- Don't date with the goal of finding your next husband. Date with the goal of finding companionship. It is much more relaxing when you are spending time with someone you like to be around as opposed to going through your "husband/wife material checklist."

- Check in often with yourself and identify what you would consider your "non-negotiables" in relationships. Stay committed to them. Stay true to them. Be true to yourself and do not settle.

There is a great chance that you are so into your rediscovery process, refocusing on your career, bonding with your children that you have no interest in dating at all. That is perfect. There is just one word of caution: Beware of those who want to constantly ask you if you have a boyfriend yet or have you started dating. People take the fact that someone is not back into the dating scene to mean that they are still pining over their lost love. This is where you communications skills come in again.

Develop a statement that you will use when the subject comes up. It needs to be a statement that says "I own my decisions" so something along the lines of, "I just don't feel the need right now" won't cut it. While it may say what you want it to say, it will leave doubt in the mind of the listener. A power statement would be more along the lines of "I am so happy where I am at right now that dating is not even on my radar." Should that be met with a comment such as "but it is healthy to start dating" then your reply should recognize what they said and restate your original comment, "I know many people think it is healthy to jump back into dating but for me…. I am so happy right now that dating is not even on my radar"… see how that works. Keep that up and eventually they will get so tired they will stop asking.

Keep in mind that it is the new empowered you that is now single not the old you. You have defined goals, have healthy habits and have clear visions. Oh how wonderful that feels!

My Story

When I reentered the dating scene, I was excited to do so as my reclaimed self. Unfortunately, I found that some of my old habits came creeping back. They did. I admit it. I was feeling great about myself. I was clear about the things that I needed to release but then found myself feeling the need to be a "pleaser." Regrettably, I didn't catch myself in time before making a huge dating mistake. I went out with a guy who was an amazing dad. He worked so hard and I admired him for that. But then I started to feel sorry for the situation he was in and like an idiot, I let him borrow money. Needless to say that is when everything in the relationship shifted. The lesson to learn is that mistakes will happen; old habits will resurface but do not beat yourself up when they do. Identify them, revisit your detox, get up, dust off and move forward.

Chapter 34:

The Detox Is a Constant Work in Progress

Do not be discouraged when you hear that detox is not a start and finish process. It is a constant work in progress and that is an excellent thing. If you were to learn to paint, cook, mountain climb or scuba dive, you would be so excited to learn the basics. It would be an awesome new skill to have but would you want to stop there? Probably not. You would want to learn more advanced painting techniques, cook bigger and better meals, climb taller mountains and dive deeper seas. Well guess what my friend? That is what detox is all about. It is about learning to cleanse yourself of toxic things in your life, learning to discover new things about yourself and learning what you have to offer to the world. Do not become complacent and revert back to the comfortable old habits even though they may seem easier.

How do you know when you are becoming complacent? The same four words that we talked about in chapter one…. Listen to your gut! Is there something that you are doing or someone in your life that just doesn't feel right? If the answer is yes then it is time to ask yourself some questions:

Am I being true to myself; staying true to my values?

This is where you need to revisit your Identity Statement. Are the things that you are doing and the people you are surrounding yourself with complimentary to your Identity Statement or are they contradictory.

Am I really living my word; am I committed to myself and others?

We all know how it feels when someone commits to something and then fails to follow through. So ask yourself: "Are there any areas in my life: personal or business, in which I have not completed what I said I was going to do?" Are you being respectful of yourself and of others? Are you living the higher standard that you have set for yourself? Again, you may want to revisit your Identity Statement.

Is that feeling of revitalization diminishing when certain circumstances or interactions occur?

This is where your gut feeling surfaces. If someone treats you in a way that you feel is not in alignment with your values, your energy will shift. That feeling of exuberance of a transformed life all of a sudden becomes heavy and encumbered. This is an instant red flag. It may have been okay in the past for you to compromise and live with the "discomfort" but the revitalized you will say that it is no longer acceptable! Now that you know how to recognize the signs, it is time to do something about it. It may mean that you need to let go of a new relationship and that is okay. Staying mentally and physically healthy is something you cannot afford to compromise. No longer will you take another lesson from the "School of Hard Knocks."

The bad news is that not every relationship in your life is going to be perfect. I am not only referring to romantic relationships but also to relationships with your friends, family and colleagues. The good news is that you now know the signs and you know how to detox. The key is to not push down or repress your emotions. Do not turn a blind eye or brush things under the rug. You are now the expert in conditioning yourself to replace the old thoughts and patterns with the new ones. You now know what it feels like when you experience the freedom and empowerment of a life of fulfillment.

Your Drama Free Divorce Detox book and Drama Free Divorce Detox Facebook and Twitter support system are here for you now and always. Do not be afraid to pick up the book and reread a chapter. Make it a habit to re-do some of the exercises. Revisit your Identity Statement regularly. Keep an ongoing ever-changing vision board. Detox and cleanse your body as well as your mind. Do something (like yoga) to nurture your mind-body connection.

All the tools are at your disposal and you are an amazing carpenter. Go out and build your dream life. A life worth living!

I wish you...

The grace of a woman

The courage of a lion

The faith of a child

~xoxo Loren

Your Go-To Resources

I. Parts of Your Body and Emotional Associations

In Chapter 14: Your body is talking. Are you listening? We visited the belief of Chinese Medicine that emotions are paired to body systems. The seven emotions related to organ function are anger, fear, joy, pensiveness, sadness, shock and worry. This chart offers a more in-depth look at each of the body/ emotion associations, its effect on the body and the standard Chinese Medicine remedy.

Emotion	Organ	Bodily Effects	Remedy (per Chinese Medicine)
Anger	Liver	Anger causes chi (life force) to escalate. This leads to the face turning red, dizziness, shaking and headache. Anger can also cause liver chi to "attack" the spleen. This will result in a lack of appetite, diarrhea and indigestion.	Various herbs can be used. It is highly suggested that coffee is avoided during treatment for liver disorder that are anger-related. Coffee is known to heat the liver which will exaggerate the condition.

Fear	Kidneys	Fear affects the kidneys and causes frequent or uncontrollable urination. Long-term fears about the future can diminish yin, yang and chi of the kidneys which can cause chronic weakness.	Treatment includes the use of yin or yang tonics to tone the kidneys.
Joy	Heart	Joy is never considered to be negative however it is the belief that too much of any stimulation (good or bad) can have negative effects on our body. Everything in moderation includes our emotions. Excessive joy can create heart imbalances which produce anxiety, insomnia and palpitations.	Acupuncture is known to correct heart imbalance. Herbal treatments are used to nourish the heart blood. Herbs known to clear heat from the heart may also be used.

Pensiveness	Spleen	Obsessing or excessive thought will deplete the spleen and cause stagnation. Symptoms include forgetting to eat, poor appetite or bloating after meals. A deficiency in spleen chi can also cause a pale complexion.	Herbal therapy is often used.
Sadness	Lungs	Sadness (grief) affects the lungs and can cause excessive crying, depression, fatigue or shortness of breath.	Treatment can include Acupuncture or acupressure. Herbs are also used to help balance the chi or yin of the lungs.

| Shock | Heart Kidneys | When shock is experienced the body reacts in a "fight or flight" manner. This reaction causes the adrenal glands to secrete excessive adrenaline. The adrenal glands are located directly on top of the kidney. This reaction also causes the heart to react with anxiety, insomnia and palpitations. | Treatment can include herbal therapy, psychotherapy and acupuncture treatments. |
| Worry | Spleen | Worry robs the spleen of energy. This results in digestive issues as well as chronic fatigue. | Moxa and herbs are used to help strengthen the spleen. This will provide the necessary energy to handle problems instead of dwelling on them. |

II. Affirmations for Healing

In Chapter 17: The Power of Positive Thinking; Affirmation Style we visited the ways that positive self-talk through affirmations can positively affect our mood, decision making and our overall health. This chart will provide you with examples of affirmations associated with particular emotions or body systems. Use these or create your own variation of the affirmation.

Help for…	Affirmation
Anxiety	"I trust the flow and process of life" "I am safe and secure" "I am calm and peaceful"
Heart	"A heart beats to the rhythm of love" "I bring joy back to the center of my heart. I express love to all" "I breathe freely & fully. I am safe. I trust the process of life" "I joyously release the past. I am at peace." "I love; I forgive; there is forgiveness in my heart."
Liver	"I am happy. I have good fortune. I am cheerful"
Spleen	"I have faith and confidence in my future; my future is secure; I am secure"
Stomach	"I digest life with ease." "I am content; I am tranquil"

Lungs	"I have the capacity to take in the fullness of life." "I lovingly live life to the full" "I am humble/tolerate/modest"
Large Intestine	"It's now okay to take in and use what I learn and know" "I am basically clean and good; I am worthy of being loved"
Small Intestine	"I am full of joy"
Kidneys	"I dissolve all past problems with ease" "I am sexually secure; my sexual energies are balanced."
Bladder	"I am freed from ideas that are no longer a benefit to me" "I let go and trust" "I welcome the new in my life" "I am at peace; I am in harmony; conflicts within me have been resolved; I am balanced."
Bowel	"I freely and easily release the old and joyously welcome the new."
Depression	"I go beyond my fear and limitations" "I give up my anger and hopelessness" "I create a life I love"

III. Never Stop Creating Your Vision Boards

While there are no rules in creating a vision/action board, if you have never created one I wanted to be sure to give you a starting point. The experience should be fun and therapeutic, no stressful. Here are a few easy steps to get you on your way.

This process can take a day or a week. Here is what you will need to get started:

- a poster board

- stack of magazines (they don't have to be current)

- glue or glue stick

- background music

Some people like to do theirs in a very quiet atmosphere and others like to create in a more fun environment.

Do not over think it! Just start flipping the pages. Tear out anything that speaks to you and represents the message of your board. You may find that you are ripping out things and you have no idea why or what they represent. That is perfectly okay. Just let it flow. Don't count how many you have or I have too many of this and not enough of that. Just cut, rip or tear anything you want to consider (you will not use all of them so don't panic).

When you feel that you are done, you can sort them in any manner you want. You can sort into piles or just lay them all out and look at what you have selected. If something pops out and doesn't feel right just discard it. No harm no foul.

Begin to lay out your selection and as you do you will start to see it come together. Again, no right or wrong, just whatever speaks to you.

When you feel ready, get your glue and start to commit the pictures to your board. When you are done, why not add some embellishments? Use stickers, dots, write with colored markers, add glitter or anything you like. Don't forget to add a personal photo if you feel it fits.

I personally like to laminate the board when I'm done. It is symbolic to me and makes me feel as if I have completed it and it is now ready to go out into the universe.

Now it is time to decide what to do with it. If it is private than display it someplace only you will see such as the inside of your closet door. Just don't keep it private because you feel silly about it or think others won't understand. It is good to let others know your goals and dreams. How else will they be able to be your cheerleader?

I like to call them action boards because when you are done it is time to act upon it. Remind yourself of what your end goal is and begin to work towards it. It doesn't need to be a huge act. If part of your goal is to start taking more "me" time then start by setting your phone alarm every night to remind you that it is time to stop washing dishes, returning email or doing laundry and time to pick up the book you have been wanting to read or drawing a nice hot bubble bath.

Remember, you are ever-changing so you action board will be ever-changing. It is a show of progress that should make you very proud of yourself.

There are many online resources dedicated to action boards. I invite you to visit my Pinterest page to view some of mine and to see the gallery of boards I have collected from other pinners.

IV. Creating Your Identity Statement

In Chapter 21: Exposing Your True Identity we visited how important a mission statement is to a business and how equally important an Identity Statement is to an individual. Be prepared to spend some time on creating your statement because anything worth creating requires thought, planning and time. The process of developing your statement will be just as beneficial as the finished product.

Here are some steps to help you get started:

Brainstorm by asking yourself these questions. Do not over analyze. Write answers in the form of lists, paragraphs or scribbles. To add a punch of fun, use a blackboard and chalk or poster board and colorful markers.

- What do I value? Loyalty? Honesty? Kindness?

- Who inspires me? What qualities do they have that I would like to possess?

- What am I passionate about when it comes to my family, my friends, my hobbies and my career?

- What do I want others to know about me?

- What is my ultimate goal in life?

Once you have brainstormed it is time to put your thoughts into a formulated statement. Here is one example of a personal Identity Statement:

Mission Statement

To remember where I have been and what I have been through and free myself from the pain by forgiving and letting go. To rebuild and maintain positive relationships with the people in my life and those who may casually pass through on their own journey. To always strive for a good work ethic. To make a personal commitment to always be honest and full of integrity. To do everything with grace and elegance. To forever pursue knowledge through education either formal or self-taught. To instill powerful values in my children so that they may grow to be adult who make a difference in the world. To be secure and content in my life by being mindful of my obligations and maintaining a healthy balance. To treat my body with respect so it will sustain me for all of my natural life. To embrace every moment of my journey, the good and the bad, with happiness, love and laughter. To remember that each day is a fresh start.

V. Recipes to Release and Rejuvenate

Throughout the book you have seen (and hopefully made) several juice recipes. Improving your health begins with the food we eat. From increased energy, lowered cholesterol, weight management and mental clarity, you can find a ton of online resources, cookbooks, self-help books and meal planning programs to help you in your quest. Here are a few more of my favorite recipes to help you release the stress from your life and rejuvenate your soul.

Island Salsa

Ingredients

- 1 - fresh pineapple: dice 1 ½ cups and squeeze 2 Tbsp. pineapple juice

- 1 –avocado; halved, pitted and cubed

- 1 - small jalapeno, seeded and diced

- 1 - Tbsp. lime juice

- 1 - Tbsp. honey

- 1 -Tbsp. extra-virgin olive oil

- 1/2 - red onion, chopped

- 2 - Tbsp. minced cilantro leaves

- Sea salt and freshly ground black pepper

Directions

In a medium bowl, mix lime honey, lime juice, olive oil, 2 tablespoons of pineapple juice and jalapeno. Salt and pepper, to taste. Mix in pineapple and onion. Fold in avocado (gently) and cilantro. Let set at least 30 in order for flavors to blend. Great on Triscuit crackers for a sweet/salty combo. Also yummy as a chicken marinade or topping.

Ginger/Lemon Tea

Ingredients

- 1" - ginger root, peeled

- 1 - large piece of lemon rind

- 1 – Juice of large lemon

- 1/3 c - honey

- 6 c - water

- 4 – tea bags (of your choice)

Directions

Slice the ginger into coin size pieces. In a small pot, heat honey, ginger, lemon rind and water; bring to a boil. Turn off heat and add lemon juice. Pour mixture over tea bags in a tea pot. Let steep 5-7 minutes. Enjoy!

Shot O' Juice

Ingredients

- 1 –carrot

- 1 – tomato, cut into pieces to fit juicer

- 1 - small beetroot (peeled), cut into pieces to fit juicer

- 2 – stalks of celery with tops

- 3 - parsley stems and leaves

- 7 – spinach or kale leaves

- 2 -coriander sprigs

Wash all ingredients and juice. Serve over ice in large shot glasses and enjoy!

Feta Salmon with Spinach

Ingredients

- ¾ lb. – Salmon Filet (cut in 2 individual pieces)

- 3 oz. - cream cheese, softened

- ½ c – chopped fresh spinach

- ¾ c – feta cheese crumbled

- 2 - scallions, thinly sliced

- Extra Virgin Olive oil

Directions

Preheat the oven to 350 F degrees.

In medium bowl, use a fork to mix (mash) cream cheese and feta cheese until blended. Mix in spinach and scallions. Spoon mixture over one piece of salmon and spread evenly. Cover with the second piece of salmon. Use olive oil to cover both sides of salmon. Bake in shallow pan for 18 – 20 minutes. Fish will begin to flake when touched with fork. Slice in half for two servings. Delicious!

VI. Ways to Celebrate the New You!

WOW! I could write a whole book on ways to celebrate the new you. There is only one rule: DO IT! Anytime you accomplish something big or small, celebrate it! Your new awareness, transformation, rediscovery, reclaiming and reinventing is certainly cause to celebrate. Here are just a few suggestions:

- Celebrate by doing something you have always wanted to do. Have you been meaning to go on that 3 mile nature walk by your house and never find the time? Have you wanted to go on a photo-cation and just explore while snapping pictures? Have you wanted to go up in a hot air balloon? There is no better time than now!

- Up the ante on girls/guys night out and do a getaway cruise. 3 day or 10 day doesn't matter. And here is a major hint: I had a friend who had 12 friends going on a cruise so she called it Girls Just Wanna Have Fun. She contacted the cruise line and booked it as a "group" versus individuals. Not only did they get free perks like cheese and fruit in their cabin each night but she got her room comped for being the "group" director.

- Clean out your closet. I know, I know... doesn't sound like a celebration at all. Oh but I beg to differ. Go through your clothes and if you haven't worn it in 12 months, it doesn't fit or you don't love it than get rid of it. Donate it. By donating you are helping others = win! By donating you feel good about yourself = win!

- Redo a space you hate. We all have the one room in our house that we aren't thrilled with, so do something about it. It is not expensive to hit up a store for a few candles, some fresh flowers, and a fresh coat of paint or a new piece of art. If you are ok with the rooms in your home than why not give your office a makeover. You spend enough time there; you should at least enjoy the way it looks.

VII.   Your Virtual Support Systems

Drama Free Divorce Detox (DFDD)

Facebook - https://www.facebook.com/dramafreedivorce-detox

Twitter- https://twitter.com/nodramadivorce

My website -http://lorenslocum.com/

VIII.   Websites to Visit

I don't need to tell you about the abundance of sites online where you can find any information about any topic. I just wanted to share a few that you may find informative and inspiring:

* **www.livestrong.com   =   food/fitness/health/lifestyle/ weight loss**

* **www.addictionblog.org = alcoholism/drug abuse/ Rx drug abuse**

* **www.kidneycoach.com =all things kidney health**

* **www.juicerecipes.com = juicing for health**

* **www.everydayhealth.com = healthy living/ drug info / healthy living / recipes**

* **www.totalbeauty.com = beauty advice/diet+health**

* **www.suzypruddenbodywisdom.blogspot.com   = affirmations/body wisdom**

* **www.bellaonline.com/articles = books/music/food/wine/ beauty/career/education**

* **www.chopra.com/articles/2010/06/18/how-to-let-go-affirmations-for-practicing-the-law-of-detachment   = emotional wellbeing/meditation/journey into healing/ relationship**

* **www.healing.about.com = holistic healing/mind, body and spirit/empowerment**

* www.mykidneycure.weebly.com/juicing-for-kid-ney-stones.html = **kidney health**

* www.rebootwithjoe.com/category/juice = a must for juicers

* www.juicerecipes.com/health/benefits/juicing-to-prevent-heart-disease = **heart health**

* www.multiculturalbeauty.about.com/od/Skincare/a/Juice-Recipes-For-Clear-And-Smooth-Skin.htm = **skin health**

IX. Special Thanks for Photographers.

Deborah Kolb

Christina Estel

Jenna Lee